Praise for She Said Yes

New York Post
It's hard to think of a book that so plainly or powerfully provides families with wisdom for surviving conflict…This book has nothing to do with the syrupy, preachy tomes typical of the "inspirational" genre. It's a profoundly human story that should be read by every parent and every teen.

Denver Post
A highly personal tale of the perils of parenting, a teenager's search for her identity, and hope…during the darkest of days.

TIME
We expect our martyrs to be etched in stained glass, not carrying a backpack and worrying about their weight and their finals. Cassie's is a mystery story, the tale of a girl lost to bad friends and drugs and witchcraft and all the dark places of teenage rebellion.

Christianity Today
A story that will chill the heart of every parent, but also bring a strong gust of hope.

Fr. Michael Scanlan, Franciscan University
Compelling…Cassie's life and death provide a model of courage and faith. It is particularly powerful given that Cassie herself emerged from the culture of hatred that engulfed her killers.

she said yes

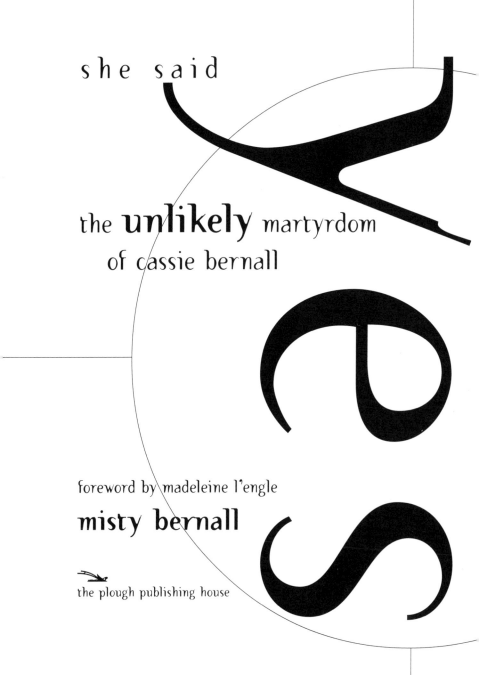

she said

the **unlikely** martyrdom
of cassie bernall

foreword by madeleine l'engle

misty bernall

the plough publishing house

First Edition 1999 (hardcover) ISBN: 0-87486-987-0
Second Edition 2002 (paperback) ISBN: 0-87486-922-6

06 05 04 03 02   10 9 8 7 6 5 4

All photographs courtesy Misty and Brad Bernall.

A catalog record for this book is available from the British Library.

Library of Congress Cataloging-in-Publication Data

Bernall, M. (Misty), 1961–
    She said yes: the unlikely martyrdom of Cassie Bernall / M. Bernall.
        p. cm.
    ISBN 0-87486-987-0 (hc.)
    1. Students – Crimes against – Colorado – Littleton – Case studies.
2. Bernall, Cassie Rene, 1981–1999. 3. School violence – Colorado –
Littleton – Case studies. 4. High school students – Colorado – Littleton –
Biography. I. Title.
HV6250.4.S78B47 1999
373.1'782'092--dc21
[B]
                                                    99-39752
                                                         CIP

Printed in the USA

To my daughter, Cassie, the little girl who brought joy to my heart, and the brave young woman whose life has touched an entire nation;

To the twelve others who perished with her at Columbine High on April 20, 1999, at the hands of two troubled classmates: Steven Curnow, Corey DePooter, Kelly Fleming, Matthew Kechter, Daniel Mauser, Daniel Rohrbough, David Sanders, Rachel Scott, Isaiah Shoels, John Tomlin, Lauren Townsend, and Kyle Velasquez;

To the countless others who suffered physical and emotional injury on that day and are still haunted by the trauma;

And finally, to my husband, Brad, and our son, Chris, whom I cherish more than ever before.

Cassie René Bernall, November 6, 1981 – April 20, 1999

"P.S. Honestly, I want to live completely for God.
It's hard and scary, but totally worth it."

*From a note written by Cassie the night before she was killed
and handed to her friend Amanda the next morning at school.*

from the publisher

Within weeks of the shooting that claimed their daughter and fourteen others at Columbine High School, Brad and Misty Bernall turned to Plough with the hope that we might help them share Cassie's story with a wider audience. The resulting book, *She Said Yes,* is based on the author's own reminiscences, on letters and notes that have turned up since her daughter's death, and on extensive interviews with classmates, friends, and other acquaintances.

Though the precise chronology of the murderous rampage that took place at Columbine High on April 20, 1999 – including the exact details of Cassie's death – may never be known, the author's description as printed in this book is based on the reports of numerous survivors of the library (the main scene of the massacre) and takes into account their varying recollections.

The Plough Publishing House

contents

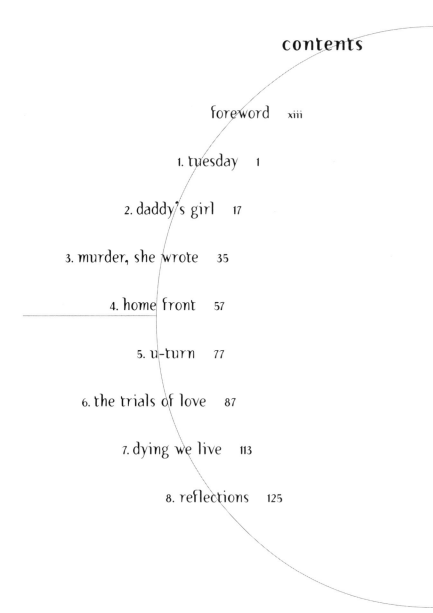

foreword

by madeleine l'engle

In a world where teenagers are constantly being accused of laziness, self-centeredness, and indifference to the needs of others, it is healing to think of someone like Cassie. Cassie is unique because we are all unique, but she is not unique in her adolescent questioning: Who am I? Does God love me and care what happens to me? Does anything I do make a difference?

Yes, Cassie, your short life has made a lot of difference. You understood that every day we have to make choices, and that the choices we make are the building blocks of who we are. Your affirmation of faith in God did not come out of the blue, but out of every choice you made along the way.

"Do you believe in God?"

"Yes."

Cassie could not have answered that question if she had not already asked it of herself many times and answered Yes many times, and each time answered it affirmatively. The Yes came deeper and deeper from her heart and mind and soul, so deep that she could say Yes even though it endangered her life. And, in the end, cost her her life.

Cassie, it seems, would not want to be labeled a martyr. There are other teenagers today who would answer the question she was asked as she did, despite the influence of friends who try to pull them away from what, deep down, they know to be true.

But even if Cassie is an unlikely martyr, her life and death – and her Yes – will never be forgotten by the students of Columbine High School, or indeed, by anybody who reads about her short life.

Do we believe in God? Yes, Cassie. Thank you.

Goshen, Connecticut
July 1999

tuesday

Sometimes a thunderbolt will shoot

from a clear sky; and sometimes,

into the midst of a peaceful family —

without warning of gathered storm

above or slightest tremble of earthquake

beneath — will fall a terrible fact,

and from that moment everything

is changed. The air is thick with cloud,

and cannot weep itself clear. There may

come a gorgeous sunset, though.

george macdonald

1. tuesday

april 20, 1999, started like any other school day in our house. At five forty-five Brad, my husband, left for work, and a little later I got up to wake the kids. Getting teenagers out of bed is always a small battle, but that Tuesday was especially difficult. Cassie had stayed up late the night before catching up on homework, and her books were all over the kitchen table. Her cat's litter box needed attention, too, and we were running late with breakfast. I remember trying not to lecture her about all the things that needed doing before she left for school…

About seven-twenty Chris kissed me goodbye, or at least gave me his cheek, which is what it's gone to lately (he's fifteen) and clattered down the stairs and out of the house. Cassie stopped at the door to put on her shoes – her beloved black velvet Doc Martens, which she wore rain or shine, even with dresses – grabbed her backpack, and headed after her brother. As she left I leaned over the banister to say goodbye, like I always do: "Bye, Cass. I love you." "Love you too, Mom," she mumbled back. Then she was gone, through the back yard, over the fence, and across the soccer field

to the high school, which is only a hundred yards away.
I dressed, made myself a cup of coffee, locked up, and drove
off to work.

Around lunchtime I got a call from Charlie, a friend,
asking me if I'd heard about some shooting at the high
school. I said no. I tried not to panic: for one thing, it didn't
seem like anything Cassie or Chris would be involved in.
Probably just some kids facing off in the parking lot, or a
drive-by on Pierce Street. For another, my coffee buddy, Val,
and I had just picked up lunch at a local market, and we
were ready to eat. Besides, I had always thought of Columbine as a safe school. Wasn't it?…I decided to call Brad, just
in case he had heard anything.

Brad was at the house when I called; he had left work
early and gone home sick. When he picked up the phone,
I told him what I had heard, and he said he had just gotten
similar news from Kathy, a friend at work. Brad had also
heard several pops outside, and one or two louder booms,
but he wasn't too concerned. It was lunch time, and there
were always kids running around outdoors. Probably just
some prankster setting off firecrackers.

After I hung up, Brad put on his shoes, went out to the
back yard, and looked over the fence. There were cops
everywhere. Back in the house he turned on the TV and

caught what must have been the first news bulletins. Shortly after that the first live coverage was aired. All at once the pieces came together, and he realized that this was no prank:

> My eyes were still glued to the tube, but I knelt at the corner of the couch and asked God to take care of all those children. Naturally, my thoughts were focused on our kids, on Cassie and Chris, but at the same time, in the back of my mind, I was sure they were both okay. It seems that if something were to happen to someone so close to you, you would sense something, feel something. I didn't.

The next thirty-six hours were pure hell. By the time I got to Columbine, hundreds of desperate parents and relatives, police officers, bomb squads, reporters, and onlookers had already descended on the area around the school, and complete pandemonium reigned.

Enough facts had emerged for us to know the seriousness of the situation, but the details were disjointed, contradictory, and confusing. All we knew for sure was that two unidentified armed gunmen had gone on a rampage through the school, mowing down students and boasting as they went. Everyone was frantically looking for someone; people were crying, praying, hugging each other, or just standing there stupidly, staring numbly as the whole chaotic scene unwound around them.

Many of the families with children at Columbine were shepherded to Leawood, a nearby elementary school, to await word from the police as to their safety; others of us were stuck at a public library, because Leawood couldn't take any more people.

It was like a battle zone. Soon lists of the injured and safe were being printed out and distributed. In between scanning the latest updates I ran breathlessly from one cluster of students to another yelling for Cassie and Chris and asking if anyone had seen them. Searching the school grounds itself was out of the question, of course. The whole campus was cordoned off and surrounded by an eerie ring of rifle-carrying SWAT teams.

Chris showed up early in the afternoon; he had fled to a neighbor's home near the high school and finally got through to Brad, who was stationed by the phone at home. Brad reached me on my cell phone. Immediately I breathed easier: Thank God; now we only have to look for one child. But the relief did not last more than a second or two, as my thoughts raced back to Cassie. *Where* was my daughter?

Though hundreds of fleeing students had been loaded into buses and driven off to safety in the immediate aftermath of the shooting, others, like Chris, had escaped the mayhem on foot, and in some cases it was hours before their whereabouts were confirmed. The injured, many of them unidentified, had been rushed off in ambulances, and dozens of others hid for hours in closets and classrooms throughout the building. Some, we found out later, were lying alone bleeding to death.

Around five o'clock those of us still waiting for news of our children at the public library were told that one last busload of students was on its way from the high school, and we should go over to Leawood to meet it. Brad and Chris had joined me earlier in the afternoon, and immediately we jumped into the car and drove toward the school as fast as we could.

Although our destination was only a few blocks away, it was a terrible drive. Nearly every street near the high school had been barricaded, and the few that were still open to traffic were clogged with TV trucks and vans from every media outlet in Denver. Overhead, TV helicopters clattered, and in front of us and behind us sirens wailed. My heart was pounding so hard, I could hardly bear the anxiety.

Finally, we got to Leawood. Jumping from the car, I craned my neck to look first one way down the street, then the other. No bus. We waited. Minutes passed, and we kept checking and rechecking the street. Still no bus. Finally, it dawned on us: there was no "last busload" coming. I was beside myself;

distraught beyond words. Up to that point I had still hoped for the best, but now? I felt deceived. Not intentionally, perhaps, but deceived nonetheless, and so bitterly that it almost choked me.

Weeks later we heard the police were certain that all the missing were dead as early as eight o'clock that evening; that they had accounted for everyone else. But because they didn't have positive confirmation, they hadn't said this, and so I continued to grasp at straws. Maybe she's hiding somewhere, I tried to convince myself. She's always been resourceful, and might have found a good place. I just hope she's not hurt. Or: It's better she's hurt than dead. If she's injured she can at least be helped. But she's *got* to make it through the night, or at least until somebody gets to her…Hope is really the only thing that will keep you going in such a crisis, even if it's a thin shred.

By nine-thirty I couldn't stand the tension any longer, and since the police were not giving out any new information, Brad and I decided to go home. It wasn't that we felt like giving up; that wasn't at all the case. But what was the point of hanging around Leawood the rest of the night? Back at the house Brad climbed on top of the garden shed in our yard. He wanted to see for himself what was going on in the school:

Standing on the roof of that shed I could see the whole school. Using binoculars I could even see right into the library windows. I could see the yellow letters stamped on the blue coats of the ATF men; they were walking around in there, heads down, as if looking for something. I couldn't really see what they were doing, but I guess they were stepping over bodies, looking for explosives. Later we heard that they found dozens of bombs…

Around ten-thirty or eleven there was an explosion from the direction of the high school. We rushed up the stairs to Cassie's bedroom to see if we could see flames or smoke or anything else from her window, but we couldn't. Nothing but blackness, and the low red and blue flashes of police cars and fire trucks on Pierce Street. It must have been a bomb detonating. I was shaking with fear and dread. What if Cassie was still alive?

Gradually fatigue overtook me, and I tried to go to sleep. It was impossible. Every time I closed my eyes, a new nightmare would jolt me awake. Again and again I saw Cassie. Cassie huddled in some dark closet, wondering if it was safe to come out; Cassie lying cold on some hallway floor, bleeding to death; Cassie crying out for help, with no one to comfort her. How I longed to hold her, to stroke her head, to wrap myself around her and hug and cry and laugh and

squeeze her tight! The agony of her absence, and the emptiness of her room, was almost more than I could take.

I had taken Cassie's pillow from her bed, and as the tears
came I hugged it and buried my face in it and breathed in
her scent. Cassie's scent. My baby's scent. I have never cried
so long, or so hard.

Around three-thirty in the morning I finally got up and
dressed, and Brad walked with me down Polk to the corner,
where the first sheriff's car was sitting. Thinking the driver
might have something new to tell us, we asked him several
pointed questions, but he only hemmed and hawed. Finally
Brad said, "Look, just tell us the truth. We have reason to
believe that our daughter is still in the school. Is anyone in
there alive?" The driver answered, "Okay, I'll give it to you
straight. There is no one left alive."

Desperate as it seems, I was still not ready to give in, even
then. There's always a chance she's hiding in a closet somewhere, I told Brad, or that she's one of the injured who wasn't
accounted for at the hospital. You never know. They think
they have their facts straight, but that doesn't mean they do.

It was twenty-two hours later, on Thursday, around two
o'clock in the morning, that my defenses finally collapsed.
The phone rang, and a woman from the coroner's office
told us what we had been dreading, though expecting, to

hear. They had Cassie's body. Now there was nothing to do but admit that our daughter was really gone forever, that she would *never* come home to me again. But how can a mother do that? I wept again, as I had never wept before.

✳ ✳ ✳ ✳ ✳

From what I have since been told, it must have been about eleven-fifteen that morning when Cassie walked into the high school library, backpack on her shoulder, to do her latest homework assignment – another installment of *Macbeth* for English class. Crystal, a close friend, was in the library too:

Sara, Seth, and I had just gone over to the library to study, like any other day. We had been there maybe five minutes, when a teacher came running in, yelling that there were kids with guns in the hall. At first we were like, "It's a joke, a senior prank." Seth said, "Relax, it's just paint balls." Then we heard shots, first down the hall, then coming closer and closer. Mrs. Nielsen was yelling at us to get under the tables, but no one listened. Then a kid came in and dropped to the floor. There was blood all over his shoulder. We got under our table, fast. Mrs. Nielsen was at the phone by now, calling 911. Seth was holding me in his arms, with his hand on my head, because I was shaking so badly, and Sara was huddled under there with us too, holding on to my legs. Then Eric and Dylan came into the library, shooting and saying things

like, "We've been waiting to do this our whole lives," and
cheering after each shot.

I had no idea who they were – I only found out their
names afterward – but their voices sounded scary, evil. At
the same time they seemed so happy, like they were playing
a game and getting a good kick out of it. Then they came up
to our table and knocked a chair over. It hit my arm, and
then it hit Sara on the head. They were right above us. I
could hardly breathe, I was so scared. Then they suddenly
left the room, probably to reload. It seemed like they had run
out of ammunition. That's when we ran for it. We dashed out
a side door of the library, an emergency exit, and made it
just before they came back in.

Crystal lost track of Cassie once the shooters entered the
room, and there are conflicting versions of what she was
doing. One student remembers seeing her under a table,
hands clasped in prayer; another says she remained seated.
Josh, a sophomore who spoke with me a few weeks after the
incident, did not see her at all, but he says he will never
forget what he heard as he crouched under a desk about
twenty-five feet away:

I couldn't see anything when those guys came up to Cassie,
but I could recognize her voice. I could hear everything like
it was right next to me. One of them asked her if she be-

lieved in God. She paused, like she didn't know what she was going to answer, and then she said yes. She must have been scared, but her voice didn't sound shaky. It was strong. Then they asked her why, though they didn't give her a chance to respond. They just blew her away.

Josh says that the way the boys questioned Cassie made him wonder whether she was visibly praying.

I don't understand why they'd pop that question on someone who wasn't. She could've been talking to them, it's hard to tell. I know they were talking the whole time they were in the library. They went over to Isaiah and taunted him. They called him a nigger before they killed him. Then they started laughing and cheering. It was like a big game for them. Then they left the room, so I got up, grabbed my friend Brittany by the hand and started to run. The next thing I remember is pushing her through the door and flying out after her…

One of the first officials on the scene the next day was Gary, a member of our church and an investigator from the Jefferson County sheriff's department:

When we got to the school they divided us up into seven teams of investigators. All of the victims who had been killed had been left in place overnight, because the investigators wanted to make sure that everything was documented before they collected the evidence.

As soon as I entered the library I saw Cassie. I knew it
was her immediately. She was lying under a table close to
another girl. Cassie had been shot in the head at very close
range. In fact, the bullet wound indicated that the muzzle
was touching her skin. She may have put a hand up to protect herself, because the tip of one finger was blown away,
but she couldn't have had time to do more. That blast took
her instantly.

✳   ✳   ✳   ✳   ✳

The gap between April 20 and the present grows a little
wider with every passing day, but the details refuse to fade.
Sometimes the images surface so vividly, it seems like it all
happened yesterday. Doctors say the brain forgets pain, and
that may be so. I am not sure the heart forgets. If there is
any reassurance to be found in the recesses of the mind, it
may be in those happy, simple things that held us together
as a family during the last week of Cassie's life. Though
uneventful in themselves, they are strangely satisfying to
hang on to, and comforting to replay.

A few weeks earlier Brad and I had taken the kids up to
Breckenridge, a nearby ski resort, for spring break, and because we still had unused tickets, we had decided to let Cassie
and Chris take a day off from school (something we "never"
do) to make use of them. So there they were, going off to

Breck on a Thursday, and as I watched them leave the house with their snowboards, I stood there thinking how my brothers and I had never done anything like that, and how special it was that my children were close enough not only to get along, but to enjoy each other's company in an activity they both loved.

Friday they both were back at school, and Saturday was prom night. Cassie did not have a date, nor did her best friend, Amanda, but both girls were determined to have a good time anyway:

> We couldn't go to the prom because we didn't have dates because we're losers, but the place where my mom works was putting on this big banquet that night at the Marriott, so Cass and I decided to dress up and do our hair and be beautiful and go there instead. We had the greatest time.

Late that Saturday night Cassie called me from the Marriott to tell me what a good time she was having with Amanda and her mother, Jill, and to say that she was planning to stop off at the house and go to the after-prom at the high school. Next thing I knew she was rattling through the house with Amanda, banging the drawers as she looked for a new set of clothes, and telling me she thought they'd be home early, because they weren't sure how it would go. As it turned out, she got home at six in the morning.

Monday was Monday. Cassie was behind on her home-work and had tons to do, because she'd been playing all weekend. Normally she babysat for friends of mine, but this week they didn't need her, so we all ate together, which isn't unusual in our home, but not something we do every night. After dinner she stayed up with her homework.

Looking back on that last evening of Cassie's life, I still see her sitting there in the kitchen. She hadn't done her chores yet, and I'm sure I nagged at her. Now that she's gone it's painful to admit. So is my belated recognition that our relationship, though generally good, was not ideal – not that night, nor any other. But it's too late to agonize over what could have been.

Perhaps the cruelest irony of losing Cassie the way we did is the fact that she never would have been at Columbine that day in the first place, had we not tried to rescue her by pulling her out of another high school, the one where she had begun the ninth grade, just two-and-a-half years before. Of course, at that time our relationship was frayed almost beyond repair, and it felt like a minor victory every time we got her home from school in one piece, let alone into the kitchen for a mundane event like a family meal or an evening of homework. But that's another chapter.

daddy's girl

daddy's girl

Many things can wait.

Children cannot.

Today their bones are being formed,

their blood is being made,

their senses are being developed.

To them we cannot say "tomorrow."

Their name is today.

gabriela mistral

2. daddy's girl

Cassie was born on November 6, 1981, no more than five or six miles from the spot where we laid her to rest seventeen years later. Our first child, she awoke in me that elemental love that will turn even the most indifferent woman into a radiant mother. More unusual than that, she turned Brad's life upside down too. There's a saying that some guys get married, have a baby, and fall in love – in that order. If it's true for anyone, I'd say it was so for Brad. But I'll let him speak for himself:

> Misty and I were married in August 1980, and by the time we had been together for three months, there was only one word on her lips: baby. She wanted a baby real bad. I wanted to hold off on having a family, and have some fun just as a couple for a year, maybe even two. But before we knew it – six months after our wedding – she was pregnant with Cassie. I wasn't as excited as a lot of men I have seen as they wait for their first one. In fact, I was even a little bit upset, because I wanted to do all these other things, and now we had this baby coming.
>
> As Misty's pregnancy progressed I was hard to live with, and hurt her feelings a lot. Looking back on it I almost

drove her away from me, because I couldn't understand why she wasn't herself; why she was tired, why she wanted (as I thought) to lie around, why she didn't feel good. I was pretty insensitive.

Then came the day that Cassie was born, and when I saw her come out of the womb – that instant – I felt like a brand new, totally different person. Suddenly I was in love with my baby daughter, and in love with my wife. Everything came together, and I understood what Misty had been going through, and I felt terrible for having given her such a hard time.

That little baby was just awesome! I wanted to do everything for her. I used to love rubbing and kissing her soft little cheeks, and her shoulders. I even changed her first diaper. Somehow that impressed the nurses, and they went out and made this little gold badge – "for being a super-dad" – and pinned it on my shirt. I was also the one who closed the lid on Cassie's casket. I wanted to be sure that it was me, and not anyone else.

When she was just a creepy-crawler, she would try to crawl after me whenever I left the house, and cry and scream at the door after I was gone. She didn't want to see me go, and I hated to leave her too. At that time I was working a twelve-hour day at Martin-Marietta, even on the weekends, and I didn't see her nearly as much as I wanted to.

In later years we had another morning ritual: I'd wake
her up around five-thirty, before leaving the house for work.
She'd be all bundled up in her blankets, and I would kiss her,
sing a little good-morning song to her, and say, "Have a good
day, Cassie, I'll see you tonight." She'd yawn and say, "Okay,
Dad."

Cassie and I loved to be together. I would get down on
my hands and knees, and we'd chase each other, crawling
through the house. I'd grab her little foot and drag her
back to me, and she'd giggle and giggle. She thought it was
so much fun. We bought her a little red wagon – a Radio
Flyer – that I used to pull her around in, and that was a real
biggie for her. She just loved that wagon.

When Cassie was about six months old I started taking
her for rides on my dirt bike. I'd put a safety belt around
myself and her, and off we'd go. I took her on some pretty
big hills – I probably shouldn't have – but she loved it. Near
the end of the ride she'd usually fall asleep, her head resting
on my forearm. We'd bounce along like that all the way home.

Misty was always nervous that I'd hurt the baby on these
rides, and I'm afraid that one time I did, though it was much
later. Cassie was about five, and Chris three, and I had them
both on the bike at once. Chris was on the gas tank in front
of me; Cassie behind me. It was muddy, and we were riding
along very slowly. I had both legs out keeping balance. We

were crawling through this muck, and I guess we hit a patch of clay. Suddenly the back wheel slid to one side, the bike tipped, and we all went down. Chris did a face-plant in the mud, and Cassie got hit by the frame just above her ankle.

After I got them out of the mud and on their feet I noticed that Cassie was standing kind of funny. She wasn't crying or acting like she was hurt, but I pushed up her pant leg a little and saw that her leg was bent. I had broken her leg. I've never felt so terrible; it just broke my heart, so I picked up both kids, mud and all, and ran all the way – it must have been several blocks – to Rick and Lori's house. They're friends of ours. Lori took Chris and put him in the bathtub and cleaned him up, and Rick took Cassie and me to the local emergency center, where we got her x-rayed (she had broken two leg bones) and bandaged up. It was a nightmare.

Misty drove over to meet us in the emergency room, and when she came in she started crying. Cassie looked at her and said, "Don't cry, Mommy. I'll be okay." Afterward, though, she was in so much pain that we sat up with her all night long.

For every anecdote I remember, Brad remembers two more. There was Cassie's first kitten, a little striped guy named Tiger that she carried everywhere, and later Jenka, a baby mallard Brad bought her one Easter, who grew to be a fine old duck that hung around the yard. We also had a mixed black Lab, Scamper, whom Cassie and Chris would ride like a horse. While Scamper lay there and wagged his tail, they grabbed handfuls of fur to hold onto him and jumped up and down.

When Brad was finishing the basement in one house we lived in, he had a big coffee can full of nails, which Cassie loved to dump out on the floor. Then, with the cat draped over her arm, she'd bend down and pick them up again, one nail at a time, and put them back into the can.

Later, in kindergarten or first grade, Brad sat her down to teach her the basics of algebra – not to push her, but just to see if she was bright enough to catch on. He explained what a set was (he'd make groups of toothpicks, forks, knives, and spoons) and she amazed us by understanding it all. After that they moved on to using letters, with Cassie adding first all the a's, then the b's, and finally the c's.

Swimming was another activity she always loved, from the very first day we put her in the splash pool we had out in the yard. As a teenager, her favorite place to swim was Glenwood Springs, a town in the Rockies with enormous pools fed by natural hot springs.

Cassie loved fishing, too, and rock climbing, an interest that caught on about three years ago on a family trip to the mountains. That was probably her favorite activity, especially after she and Chris took a class in rock climbing safety and got certified by the rec center at Breckenridge.

Looking back on Cassie's childhood, there was nothing especially unusual about it. Every mother has a warm, fuzzy feeling about when her babies were little. Now that's she gone, though, I've begun to realize the significance of every minute you spend with your child. I know it's a cliché, but it's still got some truth to it. When the kitchen's a mess, the telephone's ringing, and the kids are getting in the way, it's easy to snap or get impatient or upset. Those moments are unavoidable, but you've got to make time in between, just for your kids. Before you know it, that cute little four-year-old is a sullen teenager who won't even acknowledge your presence in the room. And in Cassie's case, at least, I don't know where we would have turned, once she was a teen, if we hadn't had a store of happy memories to fall back on. It was a place to start when we needed to rediscover our love.

✳   ✳   ✳   ✳   ✳

Memories are one thing; dreams are another. I'll start with the bad ones. It was about three weeks after Cassie's death, in early May, that I tried going to bed without a sleeping aid for the first time. It was a disaster, with one tormenting nightmare after the other all night long. At one point I saw Cassie on a gurney with her head and chest bandaged. She was smiling and talking to the paramedics who were transporting her, and telling them she was going to be all right. She really looked like she was going to pull through. Next thing I knew I was being informed that she had suddenly died after all. I could hardly stand it; I had been so sure she would live.

In another dream, I found myself shopping in a dangerous part of downtown Denver, and panicking because I needed to get Cassie out of there, quickly, to a safe place. Once I wake up from such a nightmare, it is almost impossible to get back to sleep, and I find myself debating which state is worse. I think I've decided that insomnia's the lesser evil, since when I'm awake I can at least envision Cassie the way I want to: vibrant, beautiful, and alive. In dreams her face tends to be distorted with terror as she shields herself from the muzzle pressed against her head.

Even when you know a particular fear is only a figment of your imagination, it can be hard to ignore. Just the other night the dogs were restless for what seemed like hours, growling and pawing and pacing the deck. My rational half said it was just a squirrel or a scent, but that didn't stop my heart from pounding as I lay there, listening to them and wondering whether someone was approaching the house. When the high school's just over the back fence, and they say that Cassie's killers could hardly have acted alone, you wonder how many other Erics and Dylans are still out there. At times it gets so bad that I feel ready to sell the house and move out of the area for good. Then it takes all the tenderness Brad can muster to reassure me that everything's going to be all right.

I've heard that the best way to overcome your worst fears is to face them squarely. Having done that twice in the last few weeks, I think I'm beginning to agree. Painful as it is, there's something to be said for dealing with the harsh realities of a situation head on.

First there was our visit to the cemetery. If there's anything more wrenching than seeing your own child lowered into a grave, it's going back afterward, once the bouquets are wilted and the relatives gone, to stand there alone and cry. One moment I kick myself for coming, and wish I could die on the spot, just so that I can be with my baby; the next I pull myself together and try to convince myself: you *are* with her, she sees you're here, she knows that you still love her and care about her.

One thing that strikes you at a cemetery is the way the unimportant things of life fade with time. They say that death's the great leveler, and it's really true. Most seventy- or eighty-year-olds have a lifetime of achievements behind them, whereas most seventeen-year-olds have accomplished very little. Cassie wasn't even out of high school. On the surface of it, though, the span of a life doesn't make much difference. I think it's in one of the Psalms that it says, "Behold, all flesh is as the grass…" Wherever they're from, I find a certain peace in remembering those words.

The thought of visiting Columbine High for the first time after Cassie's death was a more difficult mental hurdle. Though literally on our back doorstep, the school loomed like some strange, ominous fortress throughout the first weeks of the investigation. Sometimes I almost drove myself crazy, imagining the carnage that took place just beyond our fence. As it turned out – perhaps because I had braced myself for the worst – I was able to keep my composure.

Brad and I were the first parents to view the scene of the shootings. Rachael, our county-assigned "victim advocate," and two of the lead investigators accompanied us. There were bullet holes, splattered blood, and broken glass everywhere. In the hallways and rooms where bombs had gone off, there were gaping holes and splintered furniture, and many walls and floors were blackened by soot. In some places, melted globs of plastic from fluorescent light filters drooped from the ceiling, and there were huge, dirty puddles left by the sprinkler systems.

Throughout our grisly tour I was numb with shock, and could only gasp and stare. Afterward, though, I felt that I had accomplished something. As Brad told someone, "Now that we know what Cassie faced in her last moments, there's nothing left to the imagination. Our minds can't play tricks on us anymore."

Still, it is impossible to ever really stop wondering and worrying. At Cassie's memorial – a white tent set up by our church with candles and flowers and tables piled high with letters and mementos and gifts – someone left a large, yellow Mylar "happy face" balloon. One evening Chris was standing there with some friends and noticed that someone had taken a black marker and drawn a bullet on the balloon to make it look as if it had been shot. Sickened, Chris destroyed the balloon. But we haven't forgotten the incident. How can we?

Then there was the young man that friends of ours ran into at a local mall about nine weeks after Cassie's death. Dressed in an open black trench coat, he was sporting a T-shirt that read, "We're still ahead, thirteen to two."

It frightens me to know that after a tragedy as terrible as Columbine's, there are still people in our neighborhood who could be so brazenly cruel. How many more shootings will it take before everyone is finished with all the violence?

One thing that's been helpful to me in getting over everything is reminding myself that I am not the only one who is suffering, and trying to reach out to others who are struggling like I am. One survivor from the library, an athlete who was always a fairly confident young man, is still visibly shaken, though it's been over a month since the shooting. He is unable to look strangers in the eye, and nervously picks at his hands when he speaks.

Then there's the boy from the neighboring subdivision, a strapping sixteen-year-old who doesn't even attend Columbine, who has been having nightmares, including one in which two gunmen came into his room and sat on the edge of his bed. According to the paper, some girls in the area have so much trouble at night that they ask their mothers to sleep with them.

Strangely, it is some of the kids closest to the tragedy who have reached out to Brad and me the most. Cassie's classmates, friends from her youth group at church, and others have taken to coming over to our house to eat, talk, reminisce, or just hang out. Maybe it's the common pain we share, or the fact that we are all working through the same grief, even if in different ways. Whatever it is, their presence gives me a stability and comfort I haven't found elsewhere in my daily routine, and I sometimes find myself waiting for the doorbell to announce their arrival.

✳   ✳   ✳   ✳   ✳

I said I would write about the bad dreams first, and I have. As far as the good ones go – Cassie graduating, Cassie walking down the aisle in a bridal veil, Cassie looking forward to her own children – it hurts to say it, but it's slowly beginning to sink in: they will never be anything more than that. Just dreams.

In the months before Cassie's death we had started to talk about college, and she had grand ambitions about going to Cambridge, England, and becoming an obstetrician. I wasn't as excited as she was, especially once I found out that it cost about $30,000 a year for tuition alone. I told her, "I'm sorry, Cass. I'm afraid you've been born into the wrong family." But she wasn't going to let numbers get her down. She had fallen in love with England when she visited Brad's sister there in 1997, and she was determined to study there.

As for our dreams of her marrying and raising a family, Brad would tease her and ask, "Well, Cass, if you ever have kids, are you going to let them spend time with Grandpa? You know how I am with kids, and you know the things

I like to do." The conversation always ended the same way: "Sure, Dad, but I'm never going to get married. I'll never have kids."

✳   ✳   ✳   ✳   ✳

People say that nothing happens without a purpose – that perhaps Cassie was fulfilling a divine plan, or that in standing up for her beliefs, she was being used by God to further his kingdom. At a certain level, I take comfort in these thoughts. They give meaning to what others have called a "senseless" tragedy, and remind me that a life cut short need not be a wasted life. At another level, though, I get weary of the explanations and interpretations, of hearing about the lessons to be learned. I want to blurt out, "But why did it have to be *my* daughter?" and to tell them that no matter how deep the significance of Cassie's death, I still feel the intense pain of her loss.

Sometimes I am even frustrated by how quickly Brad has come to terms with all that has happened to us, and I get angry at him. How can he cope so easily? Brad says that he is at peace with Cassie's death, and that he is comforted by knowing she is with God. It is not that I don't share his faith. But emotions are a fickle thing, and even though I am certain that with prayer and time I will find the same

healing he has, I struggle with feelings of loneliness and
vulnerability and the temptation to despair. I am still not
where he is.

Where should I be, anyway? Is it okay to wake up crying
every morning, months after your daughter's funeral? Why,
when I·went out shopping for the first time, three weeks
after Cassie's death, did it seem that every pregnant woman
in a ten-mile radius was also there, arousing my mothering
instincts and intensifying my raw grief? Have I become un-
stable, that I can forget Cassie one moment, and yearn for her
the next? That the most trivial thing that goes wrong can
trigger a flood of tears, just when I thought I was finally
going to make it through one whole good day?

Part of it is dealing with the shock of a sudden death –
planning a funeral in your thirties for your own child, for
instance, when you didn't think you'd have to do one till
your sixties, for your parents. Or, because Columbine was
a national news story from the minute it broke, having to
respond to a steady barrage of reporters, news editors, and
photographers, on top of the stream of sympathetic well-
wishers. The first friendly call from a well-meaning stranger
might not seem like an invasion of privacy, but by the time
the twentieth comes in you're tempted to hang up on the
caller, no matter how polite he is. Everyone wants you to
talk about your daughter, and you just can't.

Later, it's the other way around: while the rest of the world moves on, you find yourself fighting the insistent desire to talk about Cassie to anyone who will listen. "I'm one of those mothers who lost a child at Columbine, don't you understand?" Even when you consciously try to turn your thoughts to the future, circumstances keep forcing you to replay the past. While I spend the morning talking on the phone with our county advocate, or petitioning the court to keep the autopsies sealed, other mothers are planning their family vacations. While the rest of the neighborhood is going to parties, I spend the evening checking Cassie's certificate of death for accuracy ("Cause of death: homicide. Type: shotgun wound to head," etc.), and worrying about what we should do with Chris in the fall. Should we send him back to Columbine? Enroll him in a private school? Tutor him at home? What's best for him? What's safest?

❋   ❋   ❋   ❋   ❋

Last night while lying in bed, trying for the umpteenth time to get some sleep, my mind returned to April 20. I am continually tormented by the thought of Cassie's final moments, of the cold panic she must have felt as a gun was held to her head. Illogical as it seems, I struggle with a sense of guilt that I was not there at her side. As her mother, I feel I let her down in the hour she needed me most. If only I had been there to stroke her, to keep her warm!

But I wasn't, and so my last gesture of maternal solidarity had to wait until the funeral home. They had wanted us to bring "a really nice dress" to lay her out in, and Cassie did have a formal or two, but she rarely wore a dress. In the end I decided on a blue shirt that she wore all the time, a pair of faded jeans, a puka shell necklace, and her Doc Martens. That was Cassie.

As for the casket, one of the first things I told the people at the funeral home was *no pink;* she's her daddy's girl. I even made sure there were no pink roses. Later, however, when we went in to look at her before the viewing, to decide whether she looked enough like Cassie to have her casket open (she didn't), the first thing I noticed was that the satin lining was pink. We debated having it replaced with a different color, but then, since we were going to close the casket anyway, we decided to leave it as it was. At times like that you don't know whether to laugh or cry. I managed to laugh. But I also promised her, as she lay there, that I had done my best. "I tried, Cass. I tried."

murder, she wrote

how sharper than a serpent's tooth it is
To have a thankless child.

william shakespeare

3. murder, she wrote

Three years ago in December, about two weeks before Christmas, I quit my job. I was working in the legal department at Lockheed Martin, where I had a full-time position, but the contract I was on was ending and it seemed a good time to break off. More important, I wanted to spend fewer hours at my desk, and more hours with my kids. Even though I had always thought of myself as a devoted mother, I wasn't finding as much time for them as I wanted. Chris's grades were slipping at school, and Cassie seemed to be growing more distant every day.

On one of the first days I spent at home after quitting my job, I was sitting there feeling blue about my inability to connect with Cassie, when I remembered that my brother and his wife had once given her a "teen" Bible – a New Testament with a sort of study guide giving young readers insights into dealing with their parents. Hoping to gain some tips myself, I wandered into Cassie's room and began looking through her drawers for it.

I found the Bible, all right, but before that I came across a stack of letters that froze me in my tracks and threw our home life into an ugly drama that was to last the next three months. Sinking weakly into the nearest chair, I began to read.

A letter addressed to Cassie from her best friend Mona (not her real name) opened with several lines of unprintable sex talk and ninth-grade gossip, and went on to discuss a teacher at the high school, Mrs. R., and invited Cassie, "Want to help me murder her? She called my parents and told them about my F." The letter ended with a reminder about a "neat spell," drawings of knives and vampire teeth, mushrooms, and a caricature of Mrs. R. lying in a pool of blood, butcher knives protruding from her chest.

Most of the other letters were decorated as well – monkeys with vampire teeth, axes, knives, mushrooms (for mind-altering drugs) – or scribbled with spells and rhymed couplets:

> Prick your finger, it is done,
> The moon has now eclipsed the sun.
> The angel of dark has spread his wings,
> The time has come for better things.

In one letter the writer went to great lengths to describe how much she hated her father; in another, how much she adored Marilyn Manson. There was endless talk about the "sexiness" of black clothes and makeup, the "fun" of contraband alcohol, marijuana, and self-mutilation, and the adventures of a classmate whose girlfriend went to "this satanic church, cult thing where you have to drink a kitten's blood to get in."

Several of the letters advised Cassie to do away with us and thus solve her innumerable problems. One ended, "Kill your parents! Murder is the answer to all of your problems. Make those scumbags pay for your suffering. Love you, me."

Another was illustrated with grisly drawings of a couple ("Ma and Pa") strung up by their intestines, daggers hanging from their hearts, and referred to the "intestine hanging thing," which the writer thought was a "pretty good idea." It then went on to say that maybe Rick (not his real name) would come up "with something even better" and gushed, "He's pretty good into this murder stuff, quite f—ed up." This letter was signed with a vampire-toothed monkey with a pentagram around its neck – Mona's symbol for herself. Still another depicted a crudely drawn knife dripping with "parent's guts," headstones for "Pa and Ma Bernall," and the letters R.I.P.

Another had a large headline, "Vampires among us forever!" followed by a crude poem:

Leave me to swallow my own blood,
Let me drink my life away.

Forever the glow of the candle shines
Through the emptiness of my soul.
Don't touch the fire, the old scar says,
My blood will boil when the right time comes.
As evil closes on my flame,
The spark of life will fade away…

"I believe I am a vampire," Mona wrote in one letter. "We are everywhere. If you kill one of us, we will get you. We are watching you constantly, beware. I am a child of the night. You are also a child of the night…I feel like burning myself. Nothing can hurt me for I am a vampire."

In another, a piece of notebook paper scrawled with drawings of marijuana leaves, vampires, moons and stars, she wrote, "My guts are hungry for that weird stuff…I f—ing need to kill myself, we need to murder your parents. School is a f—ing bitch, kill me with your parents, then kill yourself so you don't go to jail. You will go to jail."

I was flabbergasted, so dazed that I could hardly pick up the phone. But I did, and when I got through to Brad I told him I needed him to come home right away. Once he arrived at the house, we sat in stunned silence reading one letter after the next until we reached the bottom of the pile.

Most of the letters were written by Cassie's best friend, but as we later found out – both through the girl's mother and by Cassie's own admission – she too had written similar ones. In any case, the letters in our possession made it clear that even if she did not bear the main responsibility for committing the murderous fantasies to paper, our daughter was at the very least a willing accomplice.

✳ ✳ ✳ ✳ ✳

Experts say that the essence of good parenting is good guidance, and to a certain degree that's surely true. What it doesn't explain is the hard truth that sometimes – despite the best efforts of parents and relatives, teachers and friends – a good kid will go bad ways, and there is little more you can do than admit your shortcomings and start picking up the pieces. In Cassie's case, Brad and I had to recognize that there was a whole side of her life we knew very little about.

Naturally there had been signs. Though Cassie was in the ninth grade at the time we found the letters, she had been sliding away from us ever since the fifth or sixth grade, when she first began latching on to Mona and ignoring her other friends. Already at that time Brad and I were concerned about the girls' friendship, especially by Mona's inability to look an adult in the eye. There was something odd and unhealthy about their attachment.

In eighth grade, when Cassie began to toss our values and rules overboard in favor of Mona's opinions, we tried to minimize the contact between the two and encouraged

Cassie to hang out with other girls. It was useless: she always insisted that there just wasn't anyone else she was close to. And so we backed off. If there's anything a mother won't give up for a daughter, it's the hope that she will always have at least one good friend to see her through the ups and downs of high school.

All the same, I had a nagging feeling that something was not right, and no matter how many times Cassie brushed me off with, "Oh, nothing's wrong. I'm fine," I knew that wasn't the case. Still, there was nothing I could put my finger on.

Cassie was as good as any teen at playing straight. She stayed at school after hours, because "I've got to pull up my art grade" (never mind the pot smoking and the drinking, and that, contrary to what we had been led to believe, there was no supervision in the room). She showed us her cool new CD's, though not the ones she knew we wouldn't approve of. She introduced us to Rick, a classmate who seemed harmless enough, but she did her best to keep us ignorant of his dabbling in satanic rituals and his problems at home. (I later became so concerned about Rick that I went to the assistant principal about him. He acknowledged that the boy was "out of control," but said that nothing could be done: not even his parents could handle him.)

In retrospect, Cassie's change from a trusting child to a sulking stranger was so gradual that it blindsided us. It was only when we started getting calls from Beaver High School (not its real name) about her ditching classes, when unexpected D's and F's showed up on her report card, and when we caught her in one too many little lies – that we began to take things more seriously. We were losing our daughter.

One day after Brad picked up Cassie from school he came home uneasy about the occult symbols that seemed to decorate everything her friends were making in art class. Several days later, when I picked her up from another after-school art session, I grew increasingly disturbed myself. Cassie was working on her project, all right, but sitting there at the same table with her in his black garb, black eyeliner, and chain jewelry was Rick, with Mona snuggling against his chest.

Maybe it's just a mom thing, but there are times when your gut tells you there is something wrong with a situation, and you are certain it's not just because you are "out of touch" with the next generation. This was definitely one of those times. There was an oppressive atmosphere in the room, and I wanted my daughter out.

Another time I remember picking up Cassie and her girlfriends and thinking how strange it was that when Mona got into the car, she folded her arms and put her head down. She was never responsive to Brad or me – at worst, she refused to acknowledge our presence; at best, she'd mutter "hi" – but this was more than rudeness. She seemed to be giving me as hostile a signal as she dared that I was an impediment to her relationship with Cassie, and she hated me for it.

In general, Brad had better luck than I did getting through to Cassie, and she was often sweet to him. As for my relationship with her, we always seemed to be colliding about something. Cassie's ideas about music, for instance, were a frequent bone of contention in our house. During the last two years of her life she would listen to everything from the Cranberries and Pet Shop Boys to Jars of Clay and the Kry, which was fine with us, but in the ninth grade her tastes weren't half as mild. Some of the stuff she liked was enough to curl your hair.

Then again, even when you don't like the bands your child is listening to, it's not easy to put a stop to it, because "everybody else" at school listens to them. In any case, you tell yourself, you rebelled against your parents' tastes when you were in high school, and maybe this is just a phase. Maybe you don't need to get so upset about it.

I don't know exactly when it was, but at some point Brad began examining some of Cassie's music and realized that it wasn't "just" entertainment. Despite the innocuous covers, the lyrics themselves often carried an unmistakable message. (Years later we wondered whether we hadn't missed an important cue in failing to see the connection between the emotions expressed in these songs, and Cassie's own internal battles.) An excerpt from a song by Marilyn Manson, the rock group of choice among Cassie's friends at the time, and a favorite of the two boys at Columbine who killed her, is a case in point:

> …I bash myself to sleep
> What you sow I will reap
> I scar myself you will see
> I wish I wasn't me…
>
> I throw a little fit
> I slit my teenage wrist…
> But your selective judgments
> And good-guy badges
> Don't mean a f— to me
> Get your gun, get your gun…

I shudder to think where we might be today, had I not come across those letters. That was the real wake-up call.

Brad and I sat on our bed in a state of shock, reeling from the impact of our discovery. Part of me wanted to dismiss it, to say it couldn't possibly be true, that this was all a nightmare, and we would soon wake up and be able to get on with the Christmas holidays. But we were holding the reason for our worst fears right in our own hands, and we had to do something. The question was what.

In the end, it seemed clear to both of us that this was not a problem we could deal with alone, and we contacted Mona's mother, the sheriff's department, and George, our pastor at West Bowles Community Church. We also copied a set of the letters for Mona's parents, and a set for ourselves. (The originals had to be filed with the sheriff.) Then we sat and waited for Cassie.

When Cassie breezed in from school, we stopped her and told her we had found the letters. At first she tried to play it down: "Oh, we didn't mean anything bad..." Then, once she realized we were not about to let her off the hook, she flew into a screaming rage. One, we were overreacting, because she had never been serious about killing us or anyone else, and would never dream of doing such a thing. Two, we had trampled on her rights by going through her bedroom without her permission and taking things that did not belong to us. Three, since it was obvious that we had no love at all for her, our only daughter, she would relieve us of the burden by running away and killing herself. She was livid.

Cassie's defensiveness did not surprise us in the least, but it raised questions that we would have to return to over and over in the months after that initial confrontation. In the wake of her death – and the deaths of the fourteen others who died with her at Columbine – they have again come to the fore. Did we, as Cassie and Mona and her mother claimed, "blow the whole thing way out of proportion?" Didn't we, in overstepping the bounds of reasonable parenting and ignoring Cassie's "right to privacy," ask for the troubles that ensued?

On the day we discovered the hateful letters, though, there wasn't time to deliberate. We were dealing with the possibility of murder, I felt, and I was afraid for my life. In all fairness to Brad, he never took the death threats quite as seriously as I did. He felt that Cassie's flying off the handle was just her way of venting – of showing us how deeply she felt about the things she did. I wasn't too sure. When a person is gripped by an evil idea, it doesn't matter whether she's merely a troubled teenager or a dangerous adult: that evil has a power of its own. If there was even a smidgen of reality to Cassie's gory plans to do us in, I was going to make sure the sheriff knew where to start.

Even more important, we were afraid for Cassie. In fact, we were so afraid for her, we felt we had no time to stop and ponder the most appropriate response. Cassie was heading toward a cliff edge, and we had to pull her back immediately. There was no choice.

✳   ✳   ✳   ✳   ✳

After we had contacted George, he contacted Dave, his fellow pastor at West Bowles, and because it was youth night at the church, Dave suggested we bring Cassie down to join the other teens in the evening's activities. At first she didn't like the idea at all, and nor did I. I was sure she would run away or do something violent. But in the end we decided to take her. At least it would give Brad and me some time alone to gather our wits.

Later Brad went down to the county courthouse to take the sheriff the letters, while I stayed home to watch the house. I'll never forget that evening, sitting there at the dining room table with an overwhelming sense of fear and grief, thinking, "Now it's all over with Cassie. We've lost her for good." I can't recall whether I recognized it then, but I see now that we had actually lost her a long time before that.

How we managed to muddle through the next weeks I'll never know. When Cassie wasn't raging, she was seething and moody, and she continually taunted us with threats of running away. In the middle of it all I needed to have surgery. Afterwards we took the kids up to my parents' house at Grand Lake and spent a few days there, but that did little in the way of soothing anyone's nerves. It was the worst Christmas I've ever had.

Day after day, week after week, Cassie would erupt in fits of anger and despair, and we never knew quite what she would say or do next. I began to dread getting up in the morning. Brad remembers:

> When Cassie got upset with us – and I mean really upset – she would scream about how unhappy she was, and how unfair it was for us to have gone through her room. She would cry and scream and yell, "I'm going to kill myself! Do you want to watch me? I'll do it, just watch. I'll kill myself. I'll put a knife right here, right through my chest." I would try to calm her down by talking with her, or stroke her and hold her tight and tell her how much her mother and I loved her.
>
> There were times when she was acting so irrationally that I felt like slapping her, just to knock her back to her senses. But I never did. Instead I put my arms around her even tighter, pulled her real close, and said over and over, "I love you, Cassie, and I don't want to see you do anything to hurt

yourself. I don't want to see anything bad happen to you
at all."

After Cassie's death we came across an uncanny reminder
of those terrible days: a spiral-bound notebook in her bedroom with a description of the period in her own hand.
Dated January 2, 1999, it seems to be part of an unsent
letter:

> …I cannot explain in words how much I hurt. I didn't know
> how to deal with this hurt, so I physically hurt myself. Maybe
> it was my way of expressing my sadness, anger and depres-
> sion…I would lock myself in the bathroom and hit my head
> on the counters. I also did this on the walls of my bedroom.
> Thoughts of suicide obsessed me for days, but I was too
> frightened to actually do it, so I "compromised" by scratch-
> ing my hands and wrists with a sharp metal file until I bled.
> It only hurt for the first couple minutes, then I went numb.
> Afterwards, however, it stung very badly, which I thought
> I deserved anyway. I still have scars.

✳   ✳   ✳   ✳   ✳

On December 31 – New Year's Eve – we met with Mona, her
parents, an investigator, and a detective from the juvenile
crimes division. On entering the room where the meeting
was to be held, we were shocked to discover that far from

being shaken by the revelations of our daughters' friendship, Mona's parents were openly hostile toward us. When Brad crossed the room to shake hands with Mona's father, he even put up his hands and waved Brad off, saying, "Don't even bother." Throughout the entire meeting neither he nor Mona's mother volunteered anything except a muttered complaint to the effect that it was cruel to break up a five-year friendship like this.

At one point Brad made it clear that we did not feel Mona was any worse than Cassie, that both girls were equally at fault, and that we needed to work together to get through this with our girls. It was to no avail. Mona's mother admitted that the letters were not "appropriate" and that their contents made her "unhappy," but she could not understand why we had felt the need to bring them to the attention of the law, or to involve her husband in the matter. If anyone was to blame for the girls' behavior, it was us, because of our constant warnings that we would pull Cassie out of Beaver High and send her to a private school if she didn't improve her attitude.

Thankfully the detective and the investigator took the situation as seriously as we did, and supported our desire for a restraining order to bar Mona from further contact with Cassie. Among other things, the sheriff told Mona's

parents that the letters were the worst he had seen during
more than a decade in juvenile crime, and he warned them
that if Mona had had any sort of prior record, she would
have been called before a judge. Still they showed no surprise or remorse.

Brad and I were seated on one side of the room, while
Cassie sat on the other, with Mona and her parents. I can
still feel their cold, level stares. Nor will I forget how Mona's
mother walked her back to their car after our meeting, rubbing her shoulder and reassuring her, as if to say, "Oh, honey,
it's okay, the Bernalls are just mean people." Some time later
we found out that they were ready to take Cassie into their
home, should she decide to run away.

*   *   *   *   *

Needless to say, our meeting at the sheriff's office made us
more determined than ever to protect Cassie from any influence that would pull her away from us, including her own
friends. In a way, it's the hardest thing you can ever do as
parents: to put your foot down and say, "This stops right
here." Not that we thought it would be easy. We knew we
were risking an even bigger battle than the one set off by
our discovery of the letters. We knew that there was always

the chance, in clamping down on Cassie, that we would only drive her further away from us.

Yet part of me was so angry at Cassie that I almost didn't care. Here was this girl, this child I had carried for nine months and loved with all my being, telling me that she hated me! How could she betray me like this? At the same time there was no question of giving in to discouragement or admitting defeat. Brad and I had always had a certain gut feeling about what was best for our children, and we were determined to follow that feeling now. So we did.

December 20 – the day we discovered the letters – had been the last day of school before the holidays, and one of the first things we had decided was that we were not going to let Cassie go back to Beaver: from now on she would go to a private Christian school. On top of this we began regular searches of her room and backpack, monitored (or at least tried to monitor) her use of the phone, and forbade her to leave the house without our permission. Finally, we told her that she could no longer have any contact whatsoever with Mona or anyone else from their old crowd.

Cassie, of course, was beside herself with anger. So was Mona, who wrote her a note saying that we must be some of the dumbest parents in the world if we thought that pulling Cassie out of public school was going to make things any better. She was sure it would only "make things a million times worse." Besides, Mona wanted to know, how could we possibly afford private school? Didn't it cost money? The letter ended, "God, all I can say is if I had your parents they would be gone a long time ago. But enough about their revolting stupidity. Let's decide now how we should kill them…"

There was only one thing we allowed Cassie to participate in, and that was youth group activities at West Bowles. It was not church in itself that was important for us. After all, there is only one response to stuffing religion down a person's throat: rejection. Nor were we interested in trying to "save" Cassie. All we knew was this: threadbare as our relationship was, we loved her dearly, and wanted her to find a new lease on life in a place where she would not be tempted to return to her old, self-destructive ways. All we wanted was for Cassie to be truly happy, and she hadn't been up till then, not even on her own terms.

Dave (our youth pastor) still remembers the night we went over to his office to see if there was any way he could help us:

My first encounter with Cassie was a meeting with her mother and father. After reviewing the letters they had found, we sat down and talked about her, as we do many a time with the parents of kids in our youth group, or with the kids themselves. We talked about love, but also about getting real tough. I told them they had two alternatives: either you lock her in the house and cut the phone cords and all that till things are going in the right direction again, or you let things slide – hang in there till she's an adult and hope she survives.

I told them that they were welcome to bring Cassie to our youth group activities, and that we'd do our best to help her, but underneath I never gave Cassie a hope. I remember walking away from that meeting and saying to myself, "We'll give it our best, but this girl's going to be a hard one. She's gone, unreachable. There is no way that she'll ever recover from what she's doing."

Initially, it seemed Dave would be right. In a letter to a friend dated January 4, 1997, Cassie wrote:

…The letters they found in my room were really graphic, and even had pictures of how we would kill my parents. So now they know about the smoking, drinking, all that stuff, plus about our not-serious killing stuff. S——, so now I can't speak to my best friends, Mona and Judy, and my other friend, Rick. If I see or speak to Mona, the sheriff will file a restraining order. Yeah, my parents contacted the police! I think they've completely blown this whole thing out of proportion. I'm not addicted to alcohol or cigarettes. I'm not a pot-head, but basically I'm really lonely and depressed and hate my parents. Hope your life doesn't suck as bad as mine. I tried running away, but they caught me. One good thing though, I'm going to sneak out to the Marilyn Manson concert. Mona and Rick are going too, so at least I'll get to see them then.

all the vampires walkin'

through the valley

Move west

down Ventura Boulevard.

And all the bad boys

are standing in the shadows,

All the good girls

are home with broken hearts.

tom petty

4. home front

To many people, the content of Mona and Cassie's letters might seem like typical teen gossip, and in a certain way it is. Gruesome illustrations aside, it is simply a fact of life that fifteen-year-old girls do say things like "I'll kill my mother if she doesn't let us go to the mall." But where do you draw the line between idle threats and real ones?

Three weeks after Cassie's death a friend of mine talked to a student at Columbine whose brother knew Cassie's murderers. Apparently one of them, Eric, had boasted of buying the propane tanks he later used in his efforts to blow up the cafeteria, but no one had taken him seriously.

According to Annette, a friend of Cassie's who also attends Columbine, casual conversations about violence and death are so common at school that few people think twice when overhearing them. When a girl in her Spanish class talked about going to a morgue one weekend, to look at dead bodies and learn how people die, she thought it was "pretty weird," but when the girl said it was for a book she was writing, Annette relaxed. Just another person looking for attention, she thought.

A few days later the same girl came to class talking about the knives and axes she had at home, and said she wanted to bring them into school so she could show friends how she does "these cool things with fake blood." "You just don't know what to take seriously anymore," Annette says. "You think they're just saying these things to get attention, and most of them probably are. But then something happens – like with Eric and Dylan – and you begin to keep your distance."

Amanda, the classmate who was probably closest to Cassie at the time of her death, feels much the same:

I went through a stage similar to Cassie – not the witchcraft, or anything like that, but a stage where I was hanging out with the wrong crowd, just because I felt included by them. That's all I was looking for. It's loneliness: you think you're not good enough to be running with a better crowd, so you'll do anything just to be accepted somewhere, to feel like you're at least part of some group. What happened in Cassie's case, I don't know. She told me that Mona got her into it all. I don't think they sat down and made a deliberate choice like, "We're going to get involved in the dark stuff today." I can't see them doing that. But it still wasn't harmless. By the end of it she told me they were actually planning the death of one of their teachers.

During the first months after we pulled Cassie out of Beaver, it crossed my mind more than once that maybe we had been too severe with her. Since then, however, I have grown increasingly confident that we were not overly harsh.

In the late summer of 1997 in Lakewood, a nearby suburb, friends refused to believe a fourteen-year-old who said he was going to kill his parents and run off to California with his girlfriend. The next day, aided by a close friend, he attacked his father with a butcher knife and almost killed him. After the stabbing, satanic carvings and other Goth trappings were discovered in the boy's bedroom.

In September of the same year, Brad and I read of a similar incident in a local newspaper: a high school senior had shot and killed his stepfather, apparently after an argument in front of the TV set, and then gone into the garage and turned the gun on himself. Several months later there was a second child-parent murder in our area: this time the victim was a Highlands Ranch woman allegedly killed by her seventeen-year-old son and stuffed in the trunk of the family car.

In a time when supposedly peaceful middle-class suburbs like ours are breeding children capable of such things, you begin to realize that talk is never just talk. In Cassie's case, for example, it was the result of an enormous gulf of mis-communication and hostility between us – a gulf that only time, love, and attention would bridge. Even if she had really never intended to do us in, we could hardly ignore her remarks to that effect.

Now, almost three years after the fact – and in light of the shootings at Columbine – it has been a revelation for me to hear Dave's thoughts on the matter:

> Taking a kid out of school and finding him a new one, grounding him or doing whatever else you need to do to pull him up short – that might look like shutting him down. But in fact it's giving him the possibility of a whole new life. I've told that to so many parents. Many just disconnect. They say, "Well, she's already had sex five or six times," or "I know he's in with a bad crowd, but you can't stop a kid from seeing his only friends." They're worried, but they can't conceive of doing anything that will demand a sacrifice, so they pretend it isn't really so bad.
>
> In almost every case I've seen where parents take a strong stand, it's worked. It opens up a brand-new relationship. At first it's a war, because the kid's going to fight back, but deep inside his heart he's saying, "I like this. I like it that my mother's begun talking with me. I like it that my father's coming home early to see me."

Whenever I see a hurting kid, I wonder how often their
father hugs them or pats them on the back, or how often
their mother says, "I love you" or "Let me help you." Most
of these kids have parents, but are their parents really there
for them?

If anything vindicated us in the way we reacted to Cassie's
behavior, it was her own recognition of how far she had gone.
According to Jamie, a friend she first met at private school,
Cassie herself said that her violent fantasies were more than
talk. She had felt gripped by a very real power of darkness,
and it had taken her months to break free. Part of it was that
she had apparently given her soul to Satan. "I don't know
whether it was real or just symbolic," Jamie told me recently.
"But that doesn't make any difference. In her mind she had
really put herself in such a bondage."

In an autobiographical essay Cassie wrote for English
class earlier this year, she admitted, "Throughout this time
I hated my parents and God with the deepest, darkest hatred. There are no words that can accurately describe the
blackness I felt…" Though Brad and I first saw this essay
only after Cassie's death, neither of us was surprised. We
had sensed all along that there was something truly evil at
work in Cassie and her friends.

One thing I will never forget from the day we found the letters was pacing the house, praying. Brad was gone at the sheriff, and his mother had once said something about going through each and every room in the home, and asking God for his protection. I had thought it was a little odd at the time, but since I was desperate, I did it anyway. I remember coming to the doorway of Cassie's room and not being able to bring myself to walk in. I can't quite describe it, but it felt like you could almost cut the air in that room with a knife, the atmosphere was so oppressive.

Finally I went in, and I sat down on Cassie's bed and began to cry. I cried and cried, but I also prayed for God's protection over my daughter and all of her troubled friends. If there was anything I felt certain of at that moment, it was that we were dealing with more than a bunch of rebellious teenagers. Unfashionable as it might be to suggest it, I felt that we were engaged in a spiritual battle.

✳   ✳   ✳   ✳   ✳

As days turned to weeks, and then to months, our struggle to win Cassie's cooperation developed into an all-out war. The biggest obstacle in our relationship remained her insistence that, in using her letters against her (as she put it), we had trampled on her rights. But we stuck to our guns. Brad repeatedly assured Cassie that we knew she wasn't stupid; she was simply not mature enough to make good decisions on her own. He told her:

> Look, Cassie. You've got to believe that there are other ways to solve your problems. Before all this you were hanging out with a young lady who told you you'd have to kill us, and now you say you're going to kill yourself. That's not very smart…
>
> You're not dumb, but you're not being rational. When you were little, you couldn't see the burners on top of the stove. We told you that if you put your hand up there, you were going to get burned, and you had to take our word for it. It's the same now. There are things you can't see and don't understand, and you'll just have to take my word for it. You've just got to trust us, Cassie. You've got to believe that we love you and that we're never going to steer you wrong.

Anyway, Brad would talk to Cassie in this way, trying to soothe her and calm her down, and sooner or later it always worked. I guess she was smart enough to understand that she was never going to get anywhere until she could pull herself together, stop the irrational outbursts, and face the facts at hand.

The other issue at stake, at least in Cassie's eyes, was her claim that we were holding her prisoner in her own home. Actually, we had told her from the start that we were willing

to give her other options if she was going to refuse to live
with us, and we offered her several alternatives. There was
England, with Brad's sister, or Grand Lake, with my folks,
or Texas, with Brad's dad and stepmother, and we had other
relatives too. She could even run away, we told her, though
she might find herself stuck in a foster home. The only thing
we would not permit her to do was move in with a friend.
But we warned her that once she made the choice of staying
with us, it was going to be on our terms, and we were not
going to budge. As Brad summed it up to her, "No freedom,
no rights, no privileges, no trust. You're going to have to start
right back at square one and earn all those things back."

✳   ✳   ✳   ✳   ✳

We had hoped that enrolling Cassie in Christian Fellowship
School would be the answer to at least some of her problems, and in the long run it proved to be a step in the right
direction. But first it made things worse. School days con-
sisted of one wearying argument after another, beginning
with my driving Cassie and Chris to CFS in the morning.
(We had pulled Chris out of his middle school the same day
we transferred Cassie, though in his case the problem was
unsatisfactory grades.)

CFS is small and well-regulated, so we knew there was little chance Cassie would be able to escape the campus. Once we picked her up in the afternoons, however, the battles would resume. At first, because we wouldn't allow her to do anything – no after-school job, no phone calls, no visits to friends – we had to monitor every step she took. It wasn't easy, and the only way we could cope was by playing emotional "tag team." When one of us was at the end of our rope, the other would take over.

If we left the house to buy groceries or run an errand, she would call one of her friends to arrange a rendezvous or try to sneak out of the house. We couldn't trust her alone for five minutes. What we ended up doing – and I know it sounds highly intrusive – was to remove every opportunity for deceit from Cassie's personal life. We went through her backpack on a daily basis; we searched her bedroom repeatedly to make sure there was nothing amiss (we found new notes); we even installed a voice-activated recording device on our own telephone. Drastic as they were, we felt that in order to save Cassie from the path she insisted on going down, we had to take these measures.

One of the first days after we had tapped the phone, we left the house for half an hour to pick up some things at

Wal-Mart, and while we were gone Cassie called her friends. When we got home we went to our bedroom, closed the door, and listened to the tape. Cassie was yelling and cursing and carrying on in the most profane language I had ever heard from her about how much she hated us. The young man on the other end of the line was talking about how miserable he was, too, and how he was planning to end his life by drinking gasoline. (At one point Chris walked in on the conversation, and Cassie screamed and cursed at him, too. As was often the case, he was caught between his loyalty to his sister and his desire to be open with us about what she was up to behind our backs – perhaps because it frightened him.)

One day some time after this I took Cassie over to West Bowles to be with the youth group, and she snuck off and went to this same friend's home. She did this more than once, and when we found out about it, we got even tighter with her. We would call Dave and say, "We know you're not a policing entity, but Cassie's begun sneaking out. If you notice she's not there – and we're going to bring her there whenever your doors are open – please let us know."

In the same English-class essay I referred to earlier, Cassie wrote about her anger and frustration at that time:

At the private school I was completely miserable, and all the other kids literally hated me, but I had to go every day, even if I was kicking and screaming and absolutely hating it…Several times I tried sneaking out to see Mona, but I always got caught. My parents decided that none of my other friends were good influences on me. Gina was suicidal at times, and Mike was my boyfriend, so of course they didn't like him. So in addition to losing my best friend and all my freedom, I was never to see or speak to any of my other friends, either.

In between Cassie's threats and fits, we continued to warn her that she was going nowhere – that her old life was over for good, that she was not going to see her old friends, or call them, and that no matter how much she hated it, she was definitely going to continue attending private school. Sometimes I would sit with her as she screamed, my hand on her knee, praying aloud until she calmed down and telling her (like Brad did over and over as well) that I loved her.

There were times when I lost my temper, because I do have a temper, but then I would pull myself together and try again. I knew that if we were ever going to truly rebuild our relationship with Cassie, we ourselves had some work to do. The issue was never cornering her, or winning the battle for winning's sake, but finding her heart, and letting her find ours. Like it or not, we had lost Cassie's trust and respect just as she had lost ours, and the route to regaining it would have to be a two-way street.

In more concrete terms, we could not only demand sacrifices of Cassie, but had to make sacrifices ourselves. For starters, I decided not to go back to work, at least for the time being. I didn't do it lightly, because I knew that staying at home was going to require a lot more of me than an eight-hour day in an office. Nothing is so grueling as giving a child your attention and time when she doesn't want it. But I knew that unless I rolled up my sleeves and got right in there with Cassie and became as fully involved in her life as I was when she was three or four or five, we would only drift further apart. (There was another angle too: in addition to dealing with the financial strain of going from two incomes to one, we had to start paying private school tuition for both kids.)

Another way we tried to regain Cassie's trust was simply by working on our relationship – by holding our tongues when we were tempted to snap back at her, by trying to encourage her rather than nag, by offering her positive incentives and setting goals rather than putting her under pressure or making sarcastic remarks. We also made a deliberate effort to work on certain "character building" basics, as Brad called them: responsibility, respect, and self-respect.

Gradually we began to see where we had failed Cassie as parents, especially in the period leading up to her most troubled phase. Whenever Cassie was rebellious, we had tried harder to win her friendship. The more she acted out, the more we bent over backward for her. In the end, we were catering to her whims and wishes far more than we ever wanted to. It was Susan, a close friend of mine who had been a rebellious teenager herself, who helped us out of this trap. She'd say, "Stop trying so hard to be Cassie's friend. You're the adult; you're her mother; you call the shots. You don't have to have Cassie's approval for everything you do. She'll just end up thinking that the world revolves around her, and that she can do whatever she wants, because you'll still love her."

Of course, it was never a question to me that we would always love our children, no matter what. But through Susan I began to see my role as a parent in a new way – as a mentor and confidant, rather than as a buddy. I stopped trying to please Cassie and make her like me, and I started trying to guide her more consistently. Unbelievably, instead of rebelling, she accepted the boundaries I set for her and even seemed grateful for them.

✳ ✳ ✳ ✳ ✳

Once Cassie's resistances began to wear down, she grew used to the idea that she was never going to go back to Beaver

High, and found out that not everyone at CFS hated her.
She even made friends. Jamie, a fellow freshman, was one
of the first students she latched on to, and I remember my
excitement when Cassie told me about her. I envisioned this
perfect little girl who would be just the right influence on
my own wayward one. But I was in for a surprise. I was picking up Cassie at CFS, and when she asked me if Jamie could
come over to the house, I said sure. Next thing I knew, there
she was.

Jamie had a short, bleached-blond haircut, and big chains
and metal beads around her neck, and she was wearing the
sort of grungy attire that alternative types buy from places
like Goodwill. Definitely not my idea of a nice Christian girl.
Still, there was something striking about her warmth and
her unselfconscious manner, and it was not hard to see why
Cassie had found a friend in her.

In the weeks after Cassie's death I contacted Jamie and
was glad to find out several things I had not known about
their relationship. Jamie remembers:

> I got to know Cassie at CFS after she transferred there from
> Beaver. How I first heard about her is, we had the same
> guidance counselor, and this woman mentioned her and
> said that if there was any way I could reach out to her it
> would be nice, because she was really struggling, really

unhappy. So one day I walked up to her to say hello and I think I kind of intimidated her, because I'm known as one of the weird ones at the school. I think she was kind of taken aback, or else she was extremely shy. But in the end we got to be good friends.

When I first met her she was like really closed off, like "Don't talk to me." She thought nobody liked her. She was just really bitter and hopeless, and she wallowed in that hopelessness. Every day I would try to reach out to her and just quietly hope and pray that she would respond. A few times we talked about God, but she told me that she had like given her soul to Satan through one of her friends. She said, "There's no way I can love God." I would tell her, "That's not the way it has to be." We generally got along pretty good, but she'd get annoyed at me once in a while because of what I said.

She was really struggling with suicide. She'd write these really dark, suicidal poems. She also had a problem with cutting herself and hurting herself. I don't know how deep that problem was, but I know she did it frequently. She'd bring this metal file thing to school with her and she and another friend would cut themselves and stuff. She also said she'd been doing marijuana.

Cassie talked a lot about how angry she was at her parents for how they had pulled her out of her old school. That was the main topic of our conversations: being angry. She'd talk about old times with her friends, and every glimpse she'd get of them, she'd come and tell me about it. Her heart was still totally with her old crowd, and she was just really angry that she had been taken away from them. Part of it, I think, was her loyalty. Cassie had an incredible sense of loyalty to her friends, and that is why it was so difficult for her to give them up.

Though Cassie grew less "loyal" to her old crowd over time, they were determined not to let go of her. In fact, they harassed her – and the rest of us – so often that we eventually had to move.

The incident that upset me most was the time Mona and her mother arranged a rendezvous with Cassie, after we had expressly forbidden the girls to see each other. Brad and I were resting in our room when Cassie came in and said that she was going to walk the dogs. I thought, "That's really odd. She never asks to walk the dogs." But we let her go. Minutes later the doorbell rang. It was my friend Susan, and she asked us if we were aware that Mona and her mother were parked at the end of the street. There was another car there, too, with Darryn and Mike (Cassie's old boyfriend) in it, and it seemed obvious to Susan that something was amiss. (Apparently they had gotten a message through to Cassie that they would be waiting for her.) Luckily we got wind of it in the nick of time and managed to put a stop to the meeting before anything transpired. I still have no idea what they were planning.

There were other incidents, too, like the time I was harassed by old friends of Cassie's in a grocery store, and the numerous hang-up calls we got at all hours of the day and night. Then there was the afternoon that several boys from her old school drove by in a white Cherokee, hanging out the windows and yelling "Murderer!" and winging full cans of soda at our house. After cleaning up the mess we decided we'd just let it go, and take it as an isolated incident.

Later that evening, however, the same boys came by the house again, in the same vehicle. This time they hurled raw eggs at the house. While I grabbed the phone and called the police, Brad hopped in his car and went off after them. He never caught them, but later the sheriff did. They were all Cassie's old friends.

We never prosecuted the boys for vandalism, but we talked to their parents. Brad told them we had nothing against their kids and didn't want to make trouble; it was just that we were trying to raise our daughter the way we thought she should be raised, and we'd be happy if they'd ask the boys to leave us alone. That calmed things down, but it still unnerved me for a long time afterward, wondering where Cassie's old friends would show up next.

So we decided to move. We loved the neighborhood we were living in, and we loved our house, but we couldn't see keeping Cassie in such a vulnerable position. We had struggled with her too long and too hard to want to take any more risks, and in any case it didn't seem fair to make life any harder for her than necessary.

Until God has taken possession of you, you cannot have faith, but only simple belief, and it hardly matters whether or not you have such a belief, because you can arrive at faith equally well through disbelief.

simone weil

5. u-turn

One day in spring 1997, about three months after Cassie had transferred to CFS, she came home and told us that Jamie had invited her to a youth retreat. Actually, Jamie had written a letter begging us to let her go, and Brad and I had talked about it, but we weren't really sure we knew Jamie well enough to say yes. Cassie finally seemed to be making some progress, yet we were still cautious and protective, and the idea of letting her go off for a whole weekend on her own seemed like an enormous risk at the time. We told her we'd have to think about it.

Part of my reservations had to do with the church that was sponsoring the event. I had been there only a few times, many years before, and I hadn't gone back, but it had struck me as a highly charged, hellfire-and-brimstone type of place. In the end, however, we allowed her to go anyway.

All weekend long I prayed for Cassie, and all weekend long I feared the worst. What if she would run away, and we would never see her again? I was very tense. In the end, everything turned out all right, although in terms of the effect it had on Cassie, we were totally unprepared. But I'll come back to that later. First I'll let Jamie tell the story from her point of view, which Brad and I heard only this summer, about six weeks after Cassie's death:

There was this youth group that I went to, which was a church group, but you could totally be yourself there. There were these Goth types, and a lot of kids who dressed like punk rockers, you know, alternative types with weird hair. I was pretty sure Cassie would feel comfortable there, because that's sort of where she was coming from. She might not want to hear everything they had to say, but I was hoping it would click. So when I heard about this retreat they were putting on, I really wanted to go and have her come along too. She didn't want to come at first, but I told her more about it, like how cool the people were, and then she wanted to. I didn't really promote the spiritual side of it at all.

When her mom and dad dropped us off at this parking lot where we were going to leave from for the weekend, I think they were a little scared, because many of the kids had dyed hair and stuff and they were trying to get Cassie away from people like that. But they let her come, and we had a really good time. She had never come to a youth group event with me before this.

We were up at Estes Park in the Rockies, about three hundred kids, I'd say. There was a nighttime praise-and-worship service. I don't remember what the guy talked about, though the theme of the weekend was overcoming the temptations of evil and breaking out of the selfish life. It was the singing that for some reason just broke down Cassie's walls. It really seemed to change her. I wasn't expecting much out of the whole thing, also not for her, because she'd always been so closed. I thought: just one weekend is not going to change her, though it could help. So when she totally broke down, I was pretty shocked.

Actually we were outside the building, and Cassie was crying. She was pouring out her heart – I think she was praying – and asking God for forgiveness. Inside a lot of kids had been bringing things up to the altar – drug paraphernalia and stuff like that; they were breaking off their old bonds.

Cassie didn't have anything to bring up to the altar, but she was pouring out all these things she felt bad about and wanting to give them all up. There was also this other guy there, and he was praying for her too. I could hear some of what she was saying, but not all of it. After that weekend, though, I can remember her telling me many times about a lot of stuff she had done, and how she regretted it, and how she was so scared that Chris would get into the same things she had. She said it had been the worst hell she'd ever been through, and she wanted to keep her younger brother from putting himself through that.

After the service Cassie and I, and this guy named Kevin, and Justin, and Erin drove for like a quarter of a mile up the road and got out and stood under the stars up in the mountains there. We just stood there in silence for several minutes, totally in awe of God. It was phenomenal: our smallness, and the bigness of the sky. The bigness of God was so real.

Later I noticed that Cassie's whole face had changed. You looked at her, and even though she was still shy, it was like her eyes were more hopeful. There was something new about her. The rest of the retreat was really good. Like from then on, when you went up to talk to her, you knew she wanted to talk. She also had good talks with the different youth leaders.

At the end of that weekend, Brad and I left Chris somewhere and went to pick up Cassie. I was still pretty nervous. Just as we got to the church, the bus got back, and I remember seeing all these kids with spiked hair hanging around and smoking cigarettes. Then Cassie arrived in a car with a bunch of girls who were exactly the type we had been trying to get her away from – or at least they looked like it. I was thinking to myself: Why on earth did we ever allow her to go off on this trip? But when Cassie got out of the car she came straight over to me. She hugged me, then looked me in the eye and said, "Mom, I've changed. I've totally changed. I know you

are not going to believe it, but I'll prove it to you." Brad
remembers:

> When she left she had still been this gloomy, head-down,
> say-nothing girl. But that day – the day she came back – she
> was bouncy and excited about what had happened to her.
> It was as if she had been in a dark room, and somebody had
> turned the light on, and she could suddenly see the beauty
> surrounding her.

In a personal essay she wrote for English class almost two
years later, Cassie recounted her weekend with Jamie:

> Luckily there was one girl from Christian school, Jamie,
> who befriended me and took me under her wing. She was
> very open-minded and accepting, something I didn't find in
> any of the other kids. She was also the only person I didn't
> refuse to listen to. Jamie told me very gently, and in such a
> noninvasive and unoffensive manner, about Christ, and
> how what had happened to me was not God's fault. He
> might have allowed it to happen, she said, but ultimately I
> had brought it upon myself. We are given a free will, Jamie
> told me, and I had chosen to make decisions I would later
> regret. I found truth in her words and began to listen…
>
> Then, on March 8, while I was on a retreat with Jamie
> and her church, I turned my life around. It was only then
> that I was really able to see where I had gone astray. I had

made bad choices, and there was nobody to blame but myself – something I had denied constantly throughout my suffering.

I was highly skeptical. We were dealing with a child who had been incredibly hateful and desperate – experimenting with drugs, dabbling in the occult, and threatening to commit suicide or run away. I told Cassie later that I had thought her new attitude might just be a ploy – that her new friends had told her to come home and say, "I've changed" and hope we'd believe her and give her some of her freedoms back. Brad, on the other hand, was relieved by the whole thing, and willing to give her the benefit of the doubt.

Dave shared my fears. At least at first, he worried that far from being "saved," Cassie had fallen out of the frying pan and into the fire. But Cassie's conversion was a very real thing for her. She didn't get out of that car saying that she'd been saved or anything like that. She wasn't at all emotional. She was very down to earth, very matter of fact: "Mom, I've changed." And it really seemed to be true. From then on, Cassie became a totally different person. She never talked much about that weekend, and we never pressed her. But her eyes were bright, she smiled again like she hadn't for years, and she began to treat us (and her brother) with genuine respect and affection.

Cassie still wore her heavy bead necklaces and her old clothes, but somehow these things didn't matter much anymore. The important thing was the change in her spirit – her gentleness, her humility, and her happiness. She seemed to have found a freedom she had never had before, and it changed the entire atmosphere in our house.

With all we'd been through in the previous months, however, it was almost too good to be true, and so for a long time I hesitated to let down my guard. "You're doing great, Cass," I'd say to myself, "but you've got to keep proving that you're not going to slide back."

the trials of love

O divine Master,

Grant that I may not so much seek

To be consoled as to console;

To be understood, as to understand;

To be loved, as to love.

francis of assisi

6. the trials of love

To someone who sees being "born again" as all there is to the Christian faith, it might be tempting to see Cassie's conversion as the sole point of her story. As her mother, I am not sure that is really the case. There is no question that the event was a life-changing one. She even regarded the date, March 8, 1997, as a sort of second birthday – the day she was "reborn." Still, I think she would agree that what came after her weekend at Estes Park was just as important as the experience itself. As a friend once put it to me, the birth of a baby is a wonderful thing, but it's only the opening act. The best part is watching it develop and grow.

For Cassie, March 8 not only meant the end of wallowing in anger and emptiness, confusion and despair, but the chance to begin a new chapter. Now life had a purpose beyond fighting back. Now there was hope.

Already before Cassie's about-face, she had begun attending the youth group at West Bowles Community Church, or WBCC, as the kids call it. Though the peers she met there were as normal as high school kids anywhere on the surface, their influence as a group had a remarkable effect on her. Before, the values we tried to instill in Cassie at home were continually undermined by the friendships she made. Now, at West Bowles, they seemed to be reinforced.

Maybe it was the evenings they went out to eat together, or the ski trips, or the ultimate frisbee games on Saturday afternoons. Maybe it was the weekly Bible studies, the books they read, the landscaping and construction projects they did for Habitat for Humanity, or simply the discussions they had. Whatever it was, Cassie was slowly drawn in and won over. Emphasize "slowly." Shauna, a youth leader at the church, remembers the first night Cassie showed up:

> She was really standoffish, she didn't want anybody coming up to her, and she didn't want anybody to say anything to her. You can sometimes tell an insecure person right off the bat when you meet them, and Cassie – well, she was one of those. She was really one of the most insecure people I've met. I knew how she felt, though, because I had been just like that when I first started coming to the youth group. My parents had made me go.
>
> I remember commenting to someone afterwards, "That girl was one tough case, don't you think?"
>
> I still see Cassie in my mind's eye, standing there in over-sized jeans, a hemp-plant necklace, and a camouflage tank top. There was this hard look on her face – you could just tell that she'd been beat up by whatever she'd been through. Even the guys seemed nervous around her. I myself was

drawn to her – she's the type of person I hurt for, because that's where I was at one time.

She came again the next week, and the next, and the next, but it was the same thing every time. Still wouldn't talk to us.

Cassandra, a close friend, has similar recollections:

Cassie wore these ball-chain necklaces and shiny blouses, and I was so scared of her. She had this intimidating image – this don't-mess-with-me attitude. Later I found out there was a real person underneath, and I became really good friends with her. I saw that this idea I had of her was probably all in my head; that she just came across that way. It's stupid, I know, but sometimes when you see a person who fits a certain stereotype, it totally freaks you out. That's such a big problem at school, if you think of guys like Eric and Dylan – to dare to leave your comfort zone and get to know people who don't look like you, or scare you.

Shauna didn't know much, if anything, about Cassie's past, but she noticed a definite hunger to fit in and be accepted for who she was.

Gradually, she loosened up. It wasn't that we worked on her. I think it was just the sum of enough experiences where she could have a good time without worrying about who she was. We went to Funplex one time to go roller-skating;

another time we went and got food. Lots of times we'd just go out to a restaurant and eat together. We tried ice-skating one time. Cassie loved doing these things.

Kids are taught to be image-conscious; they feel they can't be childlike. They're supposed to be as mature as they possibly can the second they enter high school. But from what I've seen, teens just want to be real, and they want to be with people who are real – people who are themselves and don't care what others think.

Once, maybe a year or so after Cassie started coming, I asked her what the youth group did for her. She said she didn't really know, but that the first thing she had noticed when she came – even though she hated coming – was that everybody smiled. "Everybody was happy, everybody was having a good time." She saw this joy, and she wanted it.

At first, though, I think it made her bitter. She felt that these guys and girls had something she didn't have. It was only later that instead of being angry about it, she began to look for it.

Then there was this weekend retreat she went to, and after that she really changed. It wasn't that she was suddenly a religious person, or that her vocabulary was different or something like that. Her whole character was somehow transformed. I'm not sure she even knew what all this religious stuff meant – you know, people asking her about being born again or saved or whatever. But she did know she had found something that was going to fulfill her in a way that nothing else had up till then, and if I think about it, the thing that showed it most was her smile. She began to smile.

✳　✳　✳　✳　✳

At the end of summer 1997, between Cassie's freshman and sophomore years, Brad and I allowed her to transfer from CFS to Columbine High. Cassie had a good friend who had transferred there some time earlier, and it wasn't long before she began to badger us about how much she disliked CFS, and how badly she wanted to be at Columbine.

Earlier, of course, Brad and I wouldn't have given her request a second thought. By now, however, she had been doing well for several months, and we were open to the idea. So we went to the school and investigated. We talked to other parents, and we looked at the kids. Meanwhile both Cassie and her friend worked on us together. Finally we gave in. But we warned her: if we felt the slightest bit uncomfortable about anything – if her grades began to slip, if she missed classes, if she began hanging out with the wrong crowd – that would be it. She'd find herself back in private school in a flash.

At one point Cassie claimed, "Mom, I can't witness to the kids at Christian school. I could reach out to many more people if I were in a public one." I've never doubted that she meant what she said – that her desire to "witness" to others was a genuine one. But it is also a fact that she simply found CFS stuffy, and that made the prospects of going to Columbine with a good friend even more attractive than they already were.

Whatever her motives, Cassie's classmates at Columbine say that even though she took her new-found faith seriously, she was not one to draw attention to herself by talking about it. One of them, Eliza, was a fellow junior at the time of Cassie's death:

> I wasn't surprised when I heard what happened to her on April 20. That was Cassie. And I think that what she did was really admirable – to stand up for what you believe, no matter what. But I never really knew her religious side. Like, she didn't push it on anyone. Okay, one time in class she was reading this little Bible. I asked her what she was doing, and she said, "reading the Bible." But that wasn't a part of our friendship.

Kayla, another classmate, knew nothing about Cassie's "religious side" either, but says there was something about her that made her stand out from other friends:

> I can't explain what it was about Cassie – she was just different. She was nice to everyone she talked to at school, and she never judged someone for how they dressed or looked.

I only found out that she was religious and all that after she was killed. We talked about other things, like snowboarding. I told her that I knew how to snowboard, but I couldn't turn very well, and she said, "Oh, I'll help you work on it; I'm going snowboarding next week. If you want to come along, give me a call." So we were planning on going snowboarding together. She offered to take me with her even though she didn't really know me.

Another big difference between the old and new Cassie was the change in her tastes. Before she was obsessed with death rock and vampires and self-mutilation; now she was interested in photography (her favorite photographer was Dorothea Lange) and poetry and nature. Amanda, the friend who took her out to dinner the last Saturday of her life, remembers that she also loved Shakespeare:

> She devoured it. She would spend ages in the library picking apart the language to make sure she understood it for English class. But she didn't like all of it. We were studying *Macbeth* – that's what she was reading in the library that Tuesday, because she was behind – and Cassie just didn't like it. She said it was too dark and sinister and death-oriented. Almost evil. But otherwise she loved that stuff.
>
> Another thing we had to read that she didn't like was *Candide*. She said that half of it went over her head, and

the other half she got, but didn't like, because it was so mean.
I guess it was the sarcasm she didn't like – it was just the
opposite of how she was. She would have much rather read
another Charles Dickens book, or Emily Dickinson. We studied some of her poems in English class, and Cassie was really into that.

✳   ✳   ✳   ✳   ✳

If change involves growth, it also involves struggle. In Cassie's
case, thankfully, we were spared further drama, and there
was nothing noteworthy in the last two years. She fretted
about her weight and her looks, she worried about getting
along with other kids at school and church, and she butted
heads now and then with her younger brother, her father,
or me. According to Jamie, she still missed her old friends,
too – at least for a while:

> Even though she didn't want that kind of life, she still cared
> about her friends. It would kill her every time Mike and her
> other old friends drove by her house and hollered, which
> they did quite often, at least till she started at Columbine.
> I don't know if they were intentionally tormenting her, but
> she felt like they were – they were kind of mocking the fact
> that she couldn't be there with them. They still had a hold
> on her for a long time, and she'd talk about that: she didn't
> want it but at the same time she did, because she wanted

friends. She'd talk about wanting to move to get away from the pressure.

Later, though, she began to talk about them in a different context. Instead of saying stuff like, "Oh, we used to do this and that, and it was so much fun," she'd be like, "I wish they could find what I've found, and I want them to change too." She had a whole new attitude. It was obvious that she still cared about her old friends, but now it was a different kind of caring.

Jamie says that apart from Cassie's agonizing over classmates and peers, her biggest headache was dealing with us, her parents:

> She said that she sometimes felt they didn't care about her as a person, but just about what she did. I don't know if that makes sense, but somehow, instead of caring about the actual Cassie, she felt that her mom and dad cared more about what she looked like in other people's eyes, or maybe how she reflected on them as parents. It was a struggle for her to see that her parents really did care for her.
>
> Later we kind of lost touch: she moved schools, and I went out to Oregon for a summer. But we still talked sometimes. One of the last times we talked she said that though she felt she had grown, she was still struggling with a lot of temptations. She said, "I go through the motions of faith, I go to all the Bible studies, and everyone at the youth group

thinks I'm all right, but inside it's like I sometimes feel really disconnected, and far from God."

With some friends, you have to hide things or else you'd be scared of ruining your reputation. Cassie was so real, so honest about her struggles. We could talk about stuff that bothered us, and we didn't have to look good for each other.

Like Jamie, other friends and classmates of Cassie's have told me many things about my daughter that I might never have known otherwise. In a way it's strange, getting to know some of the most intimate aspects of your child's life only after she's gone. Sometimes I even cry, just thinking about all the things I wish I'd known earlier. In the end, though, it only makes me love Cassie more.

Cassandra, a friend from West Bowles, was especially close to Cassie throughout the last year of her life:

Cassie and I sometimes talked about self-image, about how we saw ourselves. She really struggled with that at times. Sometimes she worried that she wasn't pretty enough, or she'd talk about needing to lose weight, or she'd wish she had a different personality. But even though she thought about those things, I know she never let them control her. She was always looking to God to help her out of this stuff, and just be herself.

One thing that really stands out, thinking about it now, is that Cassie never flirted. I think that's why a lot of girls could be friends with her. You see, when you have these popular girls at school who are flirtatious and smiley and super-outgoing, you can't really be friends, because you feel intimidated. You feel a little like you're in competition.

It's like that whenever you're trying hard to win somebody over to your side. You want them to like you, but you can't just be yourself, so you put on a sort of front. Cassie didn't want to be fake. No one was in competition with her, and that's totally amazing, at least for girls in our school and even our youth group.

When I think of Cassie I always think of what Saint Francis said about how you shouldn't seek to be loved as much as you should just love. That was like embedded in her. I think Cassie felt that only God was going to be able to fulfill her, and that was probably the thing that kept her from going crazy about her image or from getting caught up looking for a boyfriend, or whatever. She refused to give in, and she was determined to overcome her problems by looking past them.

An excerpt from a letter Cassie wrote to Cassandra about a year ago confirms her point:

Hey Cass!   June 28, 1998

I am just so thankful to God for everything He's done for me, as well as for others. Even when things are bad, He's stood next to me and things are a little less prone to becoming blown out of proportion by my emotions…You know,

I wonder what God is going to do with my life. Like my purpose. Some people become missionaries and things, but what about me? What does God have in store for me? Where do my talents and gifts lie? For now, I'll just take it day by day. I'm confident that I'll know someday. Maybe I'll look back at my life and think "Oh, so that was it!" Isn't it amazing, this plan we're a part of?...

In another letter to Cassandra, dated Fall 1998, Cassie wrote:

Dear Cass,

...I know I need to give it all to Christ, but it's so hard. Just when I think I'm getting the hang of giving it all up I find myself trying to take control of my life. It's spinning all around and around, and I can't grab a hold onto anything... If I could only let my pride fall, I might be able to finally find a sense of peace and let down the barrier that is keeping me from growing in God.

I need to be completely honest with myself and to God and stop thinking I can fool him – he's GOD, for crying out loud! And I can't make compromises. It's like being luke-warm – he'll spit me out if I keep it up. I can't ride the fence one day, trying to convince myself I'm just "reaching out to people" by acting "normal," and then trying to be a dedicated Christian the next. I don't want anyone to think of me as the WBCC Hypocrite...

Well, I could go on a lot longer, but I have homework and other things to do. Plus I don't want to overload your pretty little brain with Cassie Confessions.

Despite such letters, Cassandra insists that there was nothing "heavy" about their friendship.

It's not like we were all deep the whole time, or anything like that. She just liked to hang out with people. I remember going downtown once with Sara and Cassie, and Sara and I were talking, but Cassie wasn't saying anything. She was just listening. She was the kind of person who listens. She wasn't one who wanted center stage or was always asking for attention and wanting to be heard.

Another time she and I went out to finish a project I had to do for photography class. We went to Deer Creek Canyon to take nature pictures, but it was all cold and dreary, supernasty, and we ended up taking pictures of deer on a golf course – pretty cheesy, but we had a great time.

Speaking from his informal observations of Cassie over the last two years of her life, Dave says that most of the time she was just like any other girl.

We were studying this one book, *Discipleship,* and she went straight to the chapter on marriage. She was normal, all right. Other times I saw her trying to move out of that pattern, looking for something else. To me, Cassie mirrored that verse, "Seek the kingdom of God and his justice first, and then all the rest will be added to you." I think she really connected with that – putting God first, and not obsessing about her problems all day, like so many kids do.

Dave says that what impressed him most about Cassie was that she stayed in the youth group by choice:

Some of the kids we have in our youth group are so shy and insecure, they would never dare to leave. Where would they go? From what I saw of Cassie, she could have stepped right out of our church at any time and found her way into another set of friends elsewhere, like at the high school. It was truly her choice to stay with our group.

I can't explain Cassie's motives for her. She would have been justified in complaining that she wasn't popular. She could have left. But it seems that she finally said to herself: "I'm done with that. I'm not coming here to get something out of it for myself. I'm coming to contribute, to give." We discussed this in our youth group not long before April 20. If you don't start living for other people, you end up being consumed with yourself. Once you start giving, though, your emotional needs will eventually take care of themselves.

Of course it's always easier to understand that, than to really feel it. I know it wasn't easy for Cassie. She was struggling. Just the Monday before she died I met with the youth staff, and we talked about how to rope her in more. We wanted to give her more of a chance to contribute to the group, and through that help her overcome her worries about not fitting in.

Some of the kids in the youth group are A-plus personalities: they can talk, they can dance, they're the life of every party. Cassie was not. But she still hung in there. And that's why she was a hero to me – because I see Cassies every day, year after year, and so many of them just give up.

Cassie was so hungry to contribute, to do something creative, to give. And in every case like her, where a kid is lonely or a little depressed – and we have a lot of them – it seems that once you can get them to start looking out for others, they survive. Service isn't comfort. But it gives you a purpose in life, and it forces you to stop thinking about yourself.

Still, the following letter shows that it must have been more difficult than Cassie let on to keep up the brave face she was known for. Brad found it unsent in her dresser shortly after her death. Scrawled in a spiral-bound notebook, it is dated January 2, 1999, but not addressed to anyone:

> …I have become the type of person I never wanted to become. I am depressed…I never wanted to be a negative person, or to be a crybaby. I didn't ask to be or choose to

become the kind of person that people are least attracted
to. My mom always told me to think positive and smile –
people notice and are attracted to that. I wish I could, because I want to be a fun, energetic fireball who people enjoy
being around. But I am not. I don't have the sparkling personality, amazing wit, sense of humor and energy that goes
along with an optimistic attitude that people look for.

...Sometimes it feels like the people I receive the most
compliments and uplifting comments from, the people who
say they love me the most, are the very ones who push me
down...The boys at church don't even know I'm alive. However, the guys at school give me attention. I realize that for
some of them, their motivation is lust. It would be so easy
to go to them for the love that I yearn. I'm not saying that
I'm willing to go out and have sex or anything like that, but
I'm not finding friends at church or school. Up till now I
have been strong and have not given in to this need, but I'm
sometimes afraid that I can't be strong and patient with my
hurts for much longer. Please tell me what you think.

Like the letters she left behind, the books Cassie studied
with her youth group at their weekly reading session shed
light on her search for life's meaning – in particular, the
implications of living for God. Brad and I did not realize
how much these books affected her until after her death,
because she never talked much about what she read, at least

not at home. (Perhaps – as seems to have been the case at school – she felt it was more important to try to live out her beliefs, than talk about them.) Looking at them now, however, with their Hi-Liter marks and underlinings and earnest handwritten notes, the impact they had on her is obvious.

In her copy of *Bread for the Journey,* a collection of meditations by Henri Nouwen, several of the passages Cassie marked refer to relationships with family members and friends. The first is from a piece entitled "Be Yourself."

> Often we want to be somewhere other than where we are, or even to be someone other than who we are. We tend to compare ourselves constantly with others and wonder why we are not as rich, as intelligent, as simple, as generous, or as saintly as they are. Such comparisons make us feel guilty, ashamed, or jealous…We are unique human beings, each with a call to realize in life what nobody else can, and to realize it in the concrete context of the here and now.
>
> We will never find happiness by trying to figure out whether we are better or worse than others. We are good enough to do what we are called to do. Be yourself!

On another page she underlined this:

> Without the love of our parents, sisters, brothers, spouses, lovers, and friends, we cannot live. Without love we die. Still, for many people this love comes in a very broken and

limited way. It can be tainted by power plays, jealousy, resentment, vindictiveness, and even abuse. No human love is the perfect love our hearts desire, and sometimes human love is so imperfect that we can hardly recognize it as love.

In the margin next to this she added: "Don't look for human love for comfort, but seek God's love instead."

Another book Cassie marked heavily was Heinrich Arnold's *Discipleship: Living for Christ in the Daily Grind.* In this one, several of the underlinings seem to reflect something we found out about only after her death: her quiet but apparently intense battle to find freedom from the past. These are just a few samples:

Modern man thinks too materialistically; he does not see that there is a power of good and a power of evil quite apart from him, and that the course of life depends on the power to which he opens his heart...

We run into the occult again and again, especially in colleges and high schools. Nowadays occultism is often regarded as just another science to be studied...Superstitious practices such as tipping tables or talking with the dead may start innocently, but they can bind a person to Satan without his realizing it. They have nothing to do with a childlike faith in Jesus.

Christ wants those who are most oppressed and desolate to turn to his light…They are the very ones he took to himself: the evil-doers, the tax collectors, the prostitutes, the despised of men. He did not criticize those who were possessed; he freed them. But in their freeing was judgment, for darkness was revealed and driven out.

It is important for us to decide whether we want only a nice church or the way of the cross. This must be very clear to us: Jesus' way is the way of the cross…

In one chapter Cassie underlined only a solitary sentence: "All of us should live life so as to be able to face eternity at any time."

✳   ✳   ✳   ✳   ✳

Given the high emotional stakes of most mother-daughter conflicts (and ours was surely no different), Cassie's transformation could not have been more dramatic. Nor could the olive branch she offered me – *I've* changed – been braver, or more sincere. Still, we had plenty of the arguments parents expect to have with their kids about clothes on the bedroom floor, the length of showers, the availability of the car, and money.

To make Cassie into a saint would be all too easy, especially now that she isn't there to make any more mistakes.

People talk about her smile, her ability to listen, her selflessness, and her caring character. All of those qualities were
there. But it is important to add that the daughter I knew
was equally capable of being selfish and stubborn, and that
sometimes she behaved like a spoiled two-year-old. Sure,
she was long over the worst stage of adolescent rebellion,
but I was still waiting for that final emergence every mother
waits for, when a daughter reaches true adulthood and be-
comes a companion and a friend.

After we moved from our house on Queen Street, Cassie
used to moan about how she missed her old bedroom, or
carry on about how much better she liked the old house.
Frankly, the new home we found was hardly my first choice –
the kitchen was much smaller, and the whole place needed
fresh paint and new carpet before we could move in. But
there was a reason for my willingness to submit to the up-
heaval, and it angered me that Cassie could act as if we had
done it on a whim.

Wasn't it for you, I wanted to ask her, while suppressing
the urge to grab her by the shoulders and tell her it was all her
fault, that we moved out of the old house in the first place?
That we left the neighborhood I loved? That I stopped working for four months and gave up what I considered an ideal
house in exchange for a less-than-perfect one? How many
more sacrifices did she expect us to make for her?

I always got over it in the end, but now that she's gone –
now that I think of her facing those gunmen in the very
school we thought would be safest for her – it is enough
to bring the old emotions right back up to boiling point.
You can beat yourself up about what you could have done
differently, though, and you'll still never know if you did
the right thing...

Another issue was the little Bronco we had, which Brad
bought but Cassie loved to drive. She always called it "my
Bronco," and then Brad would smile and say, "No, it's my
Bronco that I let you drive. And by the way, driving is a privilege." We had made this deal with her that if she maintained
a 3.5 GPA we'd let her use it (she still needed to ask us before-
hand), and we'd pay for the gas and the insurance. Whenever her grades dropped below 3.5 (it was trig that always
pulled her average down) she'd have to start paying for the
gas and the insurance herself, until things improved. Often
as not she'd feel we were putting her under pressure.

But now that I've spilled family secrets from my own
point of view, it's only fair to let Cassie describe them from
hers, as she did in this undated letter to Cassandra:

Have you started looking at colleges and stuff yet? I haven't,
really. It's kinda scary. College is not that far away! I really,
really want to go to school in England, though I would hate
to move away from here. Plus, I don't even know if it's God's

plan for me. I have no idea what his plan is. I don't know much about anything. I was starting to do so well, getting back on track and all, but now I'm back to square one. I'm having such a hard time! I don't understand. Where is God when I need him the most? Like now?

Family life sucks, to say the least. My mom is constantly on my case. I try so hard to make her happy, and get nothing but scowls. She does nothing but order me around. I'm so sick of being her personal slave...I clean half the house each week, do laundry and other various things, and in addition I have my own life. There's church, school, tons of homework, my exercise routine, babysitting, and other things; it varies each week...

I don't have much $, as sitting kids is not much pay. But my parents still make me buy gas and pay insurance. I don't get an allowance for all the work I do. And on top of everything else, they want me to get a "real" job. Aagh!! They say they understand, but they don't. Things have changed so much since they were teenagers. They have no idea, the things I face...Well, thanks for letting me vent. I don't get to often.

Love ya, Cass.

P.S. I'm still trying to stay strong. I don't want to lose Christ.

Sour grapes aside, Cassie had her angelic moments. She could be disarmingly generous, and often was. In fact, less than a month before she died she talked about cutting off her long blond hair so it could be made into wigs for children undergoing chemotherapy. Another time she decided to give $100 to help raise funds for a human rights project our church was supporting in the Sudan. I told her, "Cassie, one hundred dollars is a big sum to give away. I know it's your baby-sitting money, but weren't you saving it?" In the end, she decided to save the money for an upcoming trip with her youth group. I still kick myself at times for not allowing her to follow her heart.

dying we live

It is easy to die for Christ.

It is hard to live for him.

Dying takes only an hour or two,

but to live for Christ

means to die daily.

Only during the few years of this life

are we given the privilege of serving

each other and Christ...

We shall have heaven forever,

but only a short time for service here,

and therefore

we must not waste the opportunity.

sadhu sundar singh

7. dying we live

Within a day of the shooting at Columbine High, the story of Cassie's exchange with the boys who killed her was making headlines across the nation, and by the next day, people began calling her the "martyr of Littleton." At first I wasn't too sure what to make of it. Cassie is my daughter, I thought. You can't turn her into a Joan of Arc.

According to the dictionary, the Greek *martyria* means "witness" and refers to someone who refuses, in the face of terror and torture, to deny his or her faith. By that definition it's not at all inaccurate to call Cassie a martyr. As a columnist wrote in the *Chicago Tribune,* Cassie "was tried and executed by a peer who represented, in some bizarre way, a youth culture steeped in violence and death." But even if Cassie's death is a martyrdom, it is an unlikely one. I say that because before she was a martyr, she was a teen.

I'm not belittling her bravery. I'm profoundly proud of her for refusing to cave in, and for saying yes to her killers, and I always will be. She had principles and morals, and she was not ashamed of them, even though it must have taken all the courage she could muster to hold fast. When I first heard what she had done, I looked at Brad, and I wondered,

"Would I have done that?" I might have begged for my life. Cassie didn't. She may have been seventeen, but she's a far stronger woman than I'll ever be.

Still, she would hate to be held up as a shining example or singled out for praise. In any case, she was not the only one to pay for taking a stand that day at the high school. After being confronted and shot multiple times, classmate Valeen Schnurr screamed, "O my God, O my God," at which one of the gunmen asked her if she believed in God. Like Cassie, Valeen said that she did; unlike her, she miraculously survived.

Rachel Scott, another classmate, seems to have been targeted for her principles too – at least that's what her friend Andrea says:

> Rachel stood up for what she thought and paid for it. She had classes with Eric and Dylan, and I heard that she told them she didn't like their gory videos, and that their violence made her sick. She herself was into making cool videos, with happy music. You never know, but maybe they were getting back at her.

According to the kids in Cassie's youth group, forty-seven of whom go to Columbine High, there were also other acts of selflessness and bravery throughout the day. In one classroom, a teacher pulled out light bulbs to darken the room and trick the shooters into thinking it was empty. One boy threw himself on top of his sister to protect her from the gunfire and take the bullets himself. Another grabbed a bomb and tossed it clear of a group of fellow students, even though he was wounded. Dave Sanders, a teacher, stood in a hallway as the gunmen approached, blocking oncoming students and urging them to run the other way to safety. Minutes later he was shot, and by the time a rescue squad got to him, he had bled to death.

Even if Cassie had acted alone, she would hate to be elevated. Like Cassandra recently told me:

I just don't know how Cassie would respond to that label, "martyr." She wouldn't have said, "I'm so unworthy" and then taken it to herself anyway, like some people do. You know, "I'm really not worthy of this, but hey – lavish it on me all you want." Not Cassie.

We were talking once a few months ago and she said to me, "You know, I don't even feel God anymore. God seems so far away. I'm going to keep pushing on, but it's really hard right now; I just don't feel him anymore." She wasn't one to fake it and say "I'm doing just fine." She was totally honest about what was bothering her, or what she was working through, which is so rare. And I've learned to value that a lot more.

We once talked about where Jesus speaks to these hypocrites, telling them that even though they look clean on the outside, it's just whitewash – they're just bones and stuff on the inside. We were talking about what hypocrisy is, and about pretending, and how easy it is to fake it. You read your Bible and talk a certain way and it's like boom – you're automatically accepted as a good Christian. Cassie couldn't take that.

People can call Cassie a martyr, but they're off track if they think she was this righteous, holy person, and that all she did was read her Bible. Because she wasn't like that. She was just as real as anybody else. With all the publicity she's getting – the stories, the T-shirts, the web sites, the buttons, the pins – I think she'd be flipping out. She's probably up there in heaven rolling her eyes at it all and going oh-my-gosh, because she'd want to tell everyone who admires her so much that she wasn't really so different from anybody else.

To lift up Cassie as a martyr, then, is unnecessary. It won't change the facts of her life. For Brad and me it is enough to know that, whatever the reason, Cassie stood up for what she believed. It is enough to know that at an age when im-age means everything, she was not ashamed to make a stand or afraid to say what she thought.

Of course, there are always more questions than answers. What if she had said no, or said nothing? Would she have been spared? What – and this seems to be the most frequently asked question – would I have done in her place? Natural as it is to worry about these things, it is not especially useful.

It is a rare person who meets death at the end of a gun, and an even rarer one who dies heroically.

The real issue raised by Cassie's death is not what she said to her killers, but what it was that enabled her to face them as she did. I'm not saying she consciously prepared herself for a terrible end. She didn't have a death wish, I'm sure, and it would be obscene to suggest otherwise. Yet when tragedy struck her out of the blue, she remained calm and courageous. She was ready to go. Why?

In one of his first Sunday services after the shootings at Columbine, Dave said that Cassie didn't just die on April 20, but died daily over the previous two years. At first, the idea seemed distasteful, even morbid, to me. Yet the more I've thought about it, the more I've come to feel that it is an important key to unlocking the mystery of her last minutes – and to understanding the path her life was taking up to then.

> Cassie struggled like everyone struggles, but she knew what she had to do to let Christ live in her. It's called dying to yourself, and it has to be done daily. It means learning to break out of the selfish life…It's not a negative thing, but a way of freeing yourself to live life more fully.
>
> The world looks at Cassie's "yes" of April 20, but we need to look at the daily "yes" she said day after day, month after month, before giving that final answer.

A few weeks later Dave and I were talking about Cassie, and he explained what he had meant by dying to oneself:

It's the same point Jesus was trying to make when he said that he who saves his life will lose it, but he who gives up his life will find it. Long before she died, Cassie had decided that instead of looking out for herself – instead of trying to get things to work her way, and wondering what life had to offer her – she was going to see what *she* could make of it.

It's not a question of doing great deeds, but of being selfless in the small things. Cassie used to come with us to a ministry for crack addicts downtown. We'd eat with the guys, and play basketball, or just hang out with them. That's what it's all about. Saying hi to someone or shaking their hand when you'd rather look the other way. Reaching out, being willing to make sacrifices for something bigger than your own happiness and comfort.

Jordan, a college-age member of West Bowles who volunteers with the youth group there, says Cassie showed this selflessness in many little ways:

Three or four weeks before the Columbine incident, I drove her to a birthday party, and there were about five of us girls standing around, talking about weight, and looks, and Cassie said she was so tired of talking about such petty things. She said she was done with it – it did nothing for anybody, except make them unhappy about how they appeared. She wanted us to stop thinking about ourselves, and be there for others, and for the important things in life.

Shauna (she's the staffer who met Cassie the first evening she came to West Bowles) remembers a similar incident:

> One day she came to me crying. She was torn up about a conversation she had had about me behind my back. I don't think she had even initiated anything. She had just heard a negative comment or some other gossip about me, and hadn't defended me, and she felt guilty about it. So there she is, two days later, coming up to me in tears and saying, "I just wanted to say that I betrayed you, and I'm sorry. I hope you can forgive me." I had never had anybody do that to me before.

Cassie wasn't confident or especially outgoing by nature, and I can't imagine how difficult it must have been for her to make herself vulnerable in this way. But she was determined to hold firm to what she knew was right, and willing to grapple with her fears and insecurities. And in the end, even if she never completely overcame these things, her assurance of who she was and what she stood for was so strong that no one could take it away from her.

✳   ✳   ✳   ✳   ✳

One day a week or so before Cassie's death we were sitting at the kitchen table, talking, and got onto the subject of death. I don't remember how. She said, "Mom, I'm not afraid to die, because I'll be in heaven." I told her I couldn't imagine her dying – that I couldn't bear the thought of living without her. She replied, "But Mom, you'd know I was in a better place. Wouldn't you be happy for me?"

At times her thinking was so mature, and her questions so searching, it put us to shame. But it's only in retrospect – through anecdotes we've heard from her friends, and through notes and letters we've come across since her death – that we have begun to realize the depth of her innermost thoughts. In one of these notes, a scrap of paper marked "1998," she writes:

> When God doesn't want me to do something, I definitely know it. When he wants me to do something, even if it means going outside my comfort zone, I know that too. I feel pushed in the direction I need to go…I try to stand up for my faith at school…It can be discouraging, but it can also be rewarding…I will die for my God. I will die for my faith. It's the least I can do for Christ dying for me.

During her last two months, Cassie spent a lot of time engrossed in *Seeking Peace,* the newest book her youth group had chosen for their weekly discussions. Written by Johann

Christoph Arnold, an author who had spoken at our church
a year or two before (and had since become one of her favorite writers), the book seemed to strike her like nothing
she had read before. According to her friend Amanda, she
couldn't stop talking about it: "Cassie was fascinated with
that book. She was always telling me about it. I didn't have
a copy, but she'd share hers with me." As usual, she also marked
her favorite passages. Here are three from the section her
youth group was planning to discuss the evening of April
20, but never did.

> Seek until you find, and don't give up. Pray, too, even if you
> think you don't believe, because God hears even the "unbe-
> liever" as she groans. God will help you through. Don't give
> up, and above all, avoid the temptations that distract you
> from what you know you really long for. If you do fall, pick
> yourself up again and get back on track.

> Something that seems to pose the greatest challenge to hu-
> man confidence is our universal fear of death. [But] even
> this threat to peace can be overcome through the assurance
> that comes from faith – and through love, which the apostle
> John says casts out fear.

> Like anyone else, [Martin Luther] King must have been
> afraid of dying, yet…he radiated a deep calm and peace.

Here was a man with no doubts as to his mission, and no crippling fears about the cost of carrying it out. "No man is free if he fears death," he told the crowd at a civil rights rally in 1963. "But the minute you conquer the fear of death, at that moment you are free…I submit to you that if a man hasn't discovered something that he will die for, he isn't fit to live."

reflections

I reason, Earth is short,
And Anguish — absolute,
And many hurt,
But, what of that?

I reason, we could die —
The best Vitality
Cannot excel Decay,
But, what of that?

I reason, that in Heaven
Somehow, it will be even,
Some new Equation, given —
But, what of that?

emily dickinson

8. reflections

When death strikes as close as it did to us, it's almost impossible to go on without it changing the way you look at your life. Sure, we all know we could die tomorrow – we could be hit by a car, or have a sudden heart attack, or whatever. But until we're hit between the eyes with the reality of that possibility, it's unlikely that we'll ever really stop to think about what it means. Maybe that's what C. S. Lewis meant when, after losing his wife to cancer, he wrote, "Nothing will shake a man, or at any rate a man like me…He has to be knocked silly before he comes to his senses." If the tragedy at Columbine did anything, I'm confident it did at least that. It was like a jolt that stopped us in our tracks and forced us to look up from the pettiness of our daily lives.

I'll never forget how, during those endless hours of waiting to find out whether Cassie was alive or dead, I told myself that if she were safe, I would do everything in my power to make it possible for her to go to Cambridge. Why had I been so quick to dampen her enthusiasm? I found myself thinking about other arguments, too, and wishing I'd given her more slack now and then. Arguments over paying for gas and buying clothes, over stains on the carpet and other such things.

While we're talking about regrets, let me tell you about the one in our garage. Last summer, while Cassie and Chris were in Chicago with the youth group, I bought myself a Ford Expedition. Cassie had complained about having to raise her own funds for the trip, and after all the sacrifices we'd made over the previous year, I was upset. I decided it was high time I did something for myself. At least that's how I justified it then. Now, the whole thing seems rather childish, and every time I drive it the size of the vehicle seems to amplify the emptiness in my heart.

Collecting Cassie's life insurance was even worse. I'd forgotten we even had the policy, until someone asked us about benefits. (It was Brad's idea, so that if something ever happened to one of the kids, we could cover funeral expenses.) We felt so awful, taking that money – as if we were profiting from the murder of our own child. What should we do with it, other than pay down our mortgage?

Far from leaving us with tidy lessons to pass on to others, Cassie's death has landed us in a never-ending jungle of conflicting emotions. Some days we make headway, and other days we get tangled, or fall down. Take feelings like revulsion and anger. It would be dishonest not to admit that I struggle

with them. Brad keeps saying that if there is one thing that
makes all of this bearable, it's the fact that Cassie's in heaven.
It's a comforting thought, sure, but it doesn't lessen the pain
of missing her. That still cuts me like a fresh wound every
time I go and sit on her bed and realize she'll never walk
into the room again.

✳   ✳   ✳   ✳   ✳

As part of the temporary memorial set up in Clement Park
after the shootings, fifteen crosses were erected: thirteen for
the victims, and two for their murderers. Not surprisingly,
a lot of people got upset about those last two crosses. One
visitor even wrote "evil bastard" on one of them. I can understand why someone would do a thing like that, but on
the other hand, it bothers me. Such anger is a destructive
emotion. It eats away at whatever peace you have, and in
the end it causes nothing but greater pain than you began
with. It also makes it that much harder for others to console you, when you're busy nursing resentment. It's not as
if I don't have those seeds in me – I know I do – but I'm
not going to let other people water them.

There's also the whole question of revenge. It's normal,
I think, to want to bite back, whether through filing a law-
suit or by other means. But in the case of Cassie's murder-

ers, we could never go after their families. Even if we did sue them and won, no amount of money is going to bring our children back. Besides, they lost children too, and it would be cruel to act as if their grief were any less than our own.

We're aware of the controversies surrounding the Harrises and Klebolds. Some people say they were negligent parents; others that they were merely distant, or naïve. How do we know? Guilty or not, we can't just write them off. Especially not after receiving a handwritten card like this one, which appeared in our mailbox about a month after Cassie's death:

Dear Bernall family,

It is with great difficulty and humility that we write to express our profound sorrow over the loss of your beautiful daughter, Cassie. She brought joy and love to the world, and she was taken in a moment of madness. We wish we had had the opportunity to know her and be uplifted by her loving spirit.

We will never understand why this tragedy happened, or what we might have done to prevent it. We apologize for the role our son had in your Cassie's death. We never saw anger or hatred in Dylan until the last moments of his life when we watched in helpless horror with the rest of the world. The reality that our son shared in the responsibility for this tragedy is still incredibly difficult for us to comprehend.

May God comfort you and your loved ones. May He
bring peace and understanding to all of our wounded hearts.

Sincerely,
Sue and Tom Klebold

Tempting as it might be for some to dismiss the Klebolds'
letter – or to wish it said more – we can't. For one thing,
it must have taken them great courage to write and send it.
For another, having lost a child ourselves in the same in-
comprehensible disaster, we can only share their anguish.

Even if Cassie were still alive, we would be able to understand their hurt and humiliation. Before she changed direc-
tions, we agonized over her in the same way the parents of
her killer surely agonize over him now. And even if we could
never compare the weight of our separate griefs, we have at
least one comfort: the knowledge that our daughter died
nobly. What balm do they have?

We can't undo what happened at Columbine, but I am
certain that we can prevent similar tragedies from happening
again. I am sure that there must be a way to reach even the
most alienated, hostile teen before it is too late – before things
have gone so far that we feel tempted to throw up our hands
and watch our worst fears come true. If I've learned anything
from Cassie's short life, it is that no adolescent, however rebellious, is doomed by fate. With warmth, self-sacrifice, and

honesty – with the love that ultimately comes from God – every child can be guided and saved. At least I will never give up that hope.

✳   ✳   ✳   ✳   ✳

One thing Brad and I were totally unprepared for after Cassie's death was the extent of its impact beyond Littleton. Letters poured in from every state, as well as from countries all over the globe – England, Jamaica, France, Germany, Australia, and Peru. At one point the flood of mail grew so large that our entire living room was swamped with gifts and letters and cards.

Scott, a seventeen-year-old from Phoenix, wrote that Cassie's death had cut him to the heart and turned his life around. A doctor in North Carolina who had long dreamed of founding a home for street children in Honduras felt moved to step up her plans, and as of this writing, her or-phanage is finally underway. In Pennsylvania, a young couple struck by Cassie's story named a new baby daughter after her.

Aided by network television and the internet, news from Littleton even made it to rural Africa. When friends of ours were traveling in an isolated area of the Sudan, they met vil-lagers who asked them about Cassie and wanted to set up a memorial for her.

Naturally, the people most deeply affected by Cassie's death were those who knew her best – her brother, her peers at West Bowles, and her classmates at Columbine. For his part, Chris has handled the loss of his sister remark-ably well. He has his hard moments, of course. He and Cassie were unusually close for siblings their age, and given the news media's interest in our family since April 20, and the constant coming and going of friends and relatives and other visitors, he's been thrust (like Brad and me) into a situation where there's little room for private grieving. Still, we've been re-lieved to see how well he's stood up to all the pressure. He's even begun to look beyond his own personal hurt, and tried to see what Cassie's death might have to say to him in terms of a lesson or a larger meaning:

> Cassie and I had arguments here or there – little rivalries – but there was never really anything huge. We were really each other's best friend. Still, now that she's gone I realize I could have treated her a lot better.
>
> One thing I had to deal with was seeing how I hurt her. I was up in her room one day about a month after she died, and I found these poems she wrote in an old notebook. One of them was called "My Brother," and it was about how I had let her down by acting like I was embarrassed by her in front of my friends. I think she saw that I liked going out

with my friends better than being with her, and that I put them before her. That poem made me feel like a jerk, because she was always nice to me. I mean, she used to drive me everywhere: she'd take me to my friend's house and to skate parks, and to youth group activities – anywhere. And then I wasn't there for her when she needed me.

So since she died, I've tried to be more like she was. I went through my CD's and got rid of the ones that didn't have a positive message. I've tried not to be negative and tried not to judge others by how they look or what they say. I'm also trying to be kinder and more giving. I guess that poem just shows how you can hurt someone without even knowing it.

Josh, the sophomore who heard Cassie's exchange with the gunmen in the library, says her death has changed his outlook on every aspect of his life:

Until that day, I just took everything for granted. I pitch for the baseball team at school, and I took playing for granted. Even hiding under the desk that day, I was thinking, "Where do I want to get shot, if I get shot, so that I can still play ball, or still walk around." Because I lived for those games. But now I look at it completely different. I still live for baseball, but now I look at it as a privilege to be able to play. And there are other things that are way more important to me now than they were before, like my family, my little brother, and my friends.

I guess I looked at being a teenager as being immortal. As never being able to get hurt that bad, and definitely never dying, at least not for many more years. Now I can't think of it that way. I have to live today to its fullest, because I realize you can leave this earth at any given point in your life. It doesn't matter how old or young you are. Before I always thought: there's tomorrow, there's no big hurry.

Crystal, the other library survivor I quoted earlier, told me recently that she is still deeply shaken by her brush with death, and surprised at how quickly others seem able to move on.

We could still die at any given moment. I thought things would change; I thought people would be closer after going through this, and stay close. But a lot of things are still like they were. After all the excitement, a lot of people have gone right back to how they were, back into their little corners.

It would be nice to say that Crystal exaggerates, but she doesn't. Even during the first weeks after the shooting, when those of us who lost children were still making daily visits to the memorials near the school, there were others who were eager to "get over all the fuss" and move on. Sometime in early June, *The Denver Post* reported that many students were "getting pretty sick of all the memorials and stuff."

"It's become a drag," one senior was quoted as saying. "I think it's time for us all to get on with our lives." The article then went on to say that "Columbine's newest alumni are looking forward to a summer off, to backpacking trips and waitressing jobs…to college, careers, and whatever adulthood brings…They're psyched for normalcy, for life after the spring most would prefer to forget."

As the mother of one of the dead, I feel deeply hurt by such insensitivity. Who doesn't wish they could move on? Who wouldn't "prefer" to forget? I, for one, would give anything to return to the normalcy of my life before April 20, when it was uprooted, shaken, and altered forever. But I can't.

Thankfully there are more people who do understand than don't – like Jordan, who visited our house several times after Cassie's death, "just to make sure you're doing all right." Jordan says that for her, April 20 changed the way she looks at just about everything:

> I've begun to think about how temporary everything is, including human life. Seeing that coffin go into the ground at the burial, and knowing that it's all going to return to dust – that really got me thinking. All of a sudden my car, my apartment, my money, my material things, and even school didn't seem so important anymore. I took a week off from college,

because it was more important for me to be with my friends
and everyone at the church. Not necessarily to talk, but just
to be together and appreciate them.

I think a death like this should shake us and wake us up.
It should get us asking, "What is important in life?" Was it
important that Cassie was in that library studying for her
next class, getting an education so she could one day get a
job? I don't think so. To me, the important thing is that she
was prepared to go at a moment's notice.

That's why I took time off to reflect. You can't just fall
back into your normal routines. I even look at my relationship with my husband differently. We try to pray together
now, every night. It's not that I'm afraid to be attached to
the people I love. You can't live in fear. But you have to be
ready to let them go at any time.

When you love a person, their life is a gift to you, and to
just go on with your life seems to me like throwing that gift
back in their face and saying, "It was nice having you around,
but I've got other things to get on to." I don't think that's the
proper way to honor a life. You don't have to be all stone-
faced and serious – "I'm just going to suck it up and be
tough." But I think it's important not to skip the reflecting.

An event like this should cut us. It should change us. If it
doesn't, there's something wrong. If you just let your life go
on like it did before, you're burying a gift you've been given.
You're missing an important moment.

Like Jordan, I feel that to try to go on with life as usual after losing a loved one is to dishonor the dead. It spells rejection of the message that death has for us, the living, and the reality of eternity, before which – when it breaks into time – we must stand silent and be still.

Reflecting is never easy. It is easier to weep, in the dark morning hours when I can't go back to sleep; to bury my face in the pillows and cry till I ache. Why? *Why?* How could they kill her? How could *anyone* do what they did, how could they treat *anyone* like that? How could they look into her sweet, young face; into her blue eyes? How could anyone be so callous as to put a gun to my daughter's head?

It is also easier to get angry, to point fingers, or to lose oneself in what the media calls the "larger" issues. In the wake of Columbine that has meant gun control and video games, school security and Hollywood violence, preventative education and separation of church and state. All of these issues are important, but at the end of the day they may not be the things that really count. Or are they?

Why, when parents and lawmakers are calling for gun control and an end to TV violence, are our young crying out for relationships? Why, when we offer them psychologists and counselors and experts on conflict resolution, are they going to youth groups and looking for friends? Why, when everyone else is apportioning blame and constructing new defenses, are they talking about a change of the heart?

The more I think about it, the more certain I am that, political and public as the broader discussion might be, we cannot forget the equally vital role of our more personal efforts to prevent tragedies like the one that claimed Cassie. To me, at least, it comes down to acting generously and spontaneously, even when caution holds me back. It means choosing to extend a hand rather than recoiling judgmentally; and following an impulse, even when (as Cassie would say) it might draw me out of my "comfort zone" and cost me something. Finally, it means daring to sacrifice all for Love's sake –not as a hero or a martyr, necessarily – but consistently and with conviction, in the small, everyday things that make up a life.

That is why I am able, ultimately, to see the loss of my daughter not so much as a defeat, as a victory. The pain is no less. It will always remain deep and raw. Even so, I know that her death was not a waste, but a triumph of honesty and courage. To me, Cassie's life says that it is better to die for what you believe, than to live a lie.

✳   ✳   ✳   ✳   ✳

A few days after my daughter's death, I learned that on April 20, while bullets wreaked havoc in the halls of Columbine

High, friends of ours traveling in Israel were attending a
service to remember fallen soldiers. As the choir chanted
in Hebrew, an interpreter explained. It was a tribute to
the country's martyrs, and the translation ran something
like this: "My death is not my own, but yours, and its significance depends on what you do with it."

If there is anything I would like to leave you, the reader, it
is the same thought: Cassie's story is not only mine and Brad's.
It is yours, and what you do with it now will give it meaning.

acknowledgments

There are so many who have supported and carried us through the tragedy at Columbine, and through the making of this book, which has emerged out of its ashes. We wish to acknowledge at least a few of them: all of the dedicated law enforcement personnel, fire fighters, paramedics, and emergency workers, both volunteer and professional; our pastors, George Kirsten and Dave McPherson; the loving and ever-giving congregation of West Bowles Community Church; our brothers, sisters, moms and dads, and our extended family in Christ (you know who you are); the people from the Plough Publishing House, who have become our friends; our neighbors; the Littleton community, and each and every one of the countless others from around the globe who have so lovingly and generously reached out to us; and most importantly, our Father, God. He himself lost a child – his son, Jesus Christ – and it is he who has given us the strength to bear our loss.

two of cassie's favorite books...

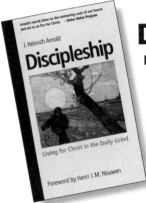

Discipleship

Living for Christ in the Daily Grind

by J. Heinrich Arnold
Foreword by Henri Nouwen

301 pages, softcover

"Live life so as to be able to
face eternity at any time."

as Cassie struggled to hold to her new-found faith, the books she studied with her church youth group had a deep impact on her – or so it seems, from the way she marked up her personal copies.

One of these books, *Discipleship*, offers hard-won insights into the challenges of living for Christ in daily life. It's no secret that the hardest thing about it is translating your good intentions into deeds. At times, you may even begin to wonder just how feasible it is in today's hectic world. How can you be centered on anything, when everything seems to pull you apart?

Topically arranged, many of the meditations in *Discipleship* address such specific concerns. Others take on broader themes. All of them pulsate with conviction and radiate compassion and hope.

TO ORDER visit our website at www.plough.com or call
1-800-521-8011 or 724-329-1100 (US)
or 0800 018 0799 or +44(0)1580 883 344 (UK)

Be Not Afraid

Overcoming the Fear of Death

Johann Christoph Arnold

222 pages, softcover

"Who hasn't felt
the grip of fear?"

fear of accidents or terrorism, illness or dying, loneliness or grief –if you're like most people, you've dealt with at least one of these anxieties before. In *Be Not Afraid,* Arnold, a seasoned pastoral counselor, relates stories of real men, women, and children who found strength to conquer their deepest fears. Interspersed with anecdotes from such wise teachers as Tolstoy, Dickens, and Dorothy Day, Arnold reassures us that even in our age of anxiety, we need not fear death, but can live life fully and with confidence.

John Dear, S.J.
Arnold challenges me to confront my own fear of death…his stories encourage me to embrace the God of life. They are a great comfort.